Hey Pup, Let's Talk!

C. Miriam Yarden, B.Sc.

BARRON'S

"There are facts about dogs, and there's opinions about them. The dogs have the facts and the humans have opinions. If you want opinions, get them from the human. If you want facts about dogs, get them straight from the dog.

"Trained animals are relatively easy to turn out. All that is required is a book of instructions, a certain amount of bluff and bluster, something to use for threatening and punishing purposes, and of course, the animal.

"*Educating* an animal, on the other hand, demands keen intelligence, integrity, imagination, and the gentle touch mentally, vocally and physically."

J. Allen Boone
Kinship With All Life

* * * *

To err is human. To forgive is canine.   —Anonymous

About the Author: Animal psychologist **C. Miriam Yarden** has been treating serious dog and cat behavior problems for families in Southern California for 25 years. She is the president of AURORA Animal Behaviour in Long Beach, CA, and she *only* makes house calls. She is also a well-respected lecturer on the subject of animal behavior, and a member of the Southern California Veterinarian Medical Association (SCVMA) and the American Veterinarian Society of Animal Behavior.

© Copyright 2000 by Barron's Educational Series, Inc.

All inquiries should be addressed to:
Barron's Educational Series, Inc.
250 Wireless Boulevard
Hauppauge, New York 11788
http://www.barronseduc.com

International Standard Book No. 0-7641-1227-9
Library of Congress Catalog Card No. 99-86410

Library of Congress Cataloging-in-Publication Data
Yarden, C. Miriam.
   Hey pup, let's talk! : actual case histories of dogs with
   behavior problems / C. Miriam Yarden.
      p.   cm.
   ISBN 0-7641-1227-9
   1. Dogs—Behaviors—United States—Anecdotes.
   2. Veterinarians—United States—Anecdotes.
   3. Yarden, C. Miriam. I. Title.
SF433.Y37   2000
636.7'0887—dc21   99-86410
                                         CIP

Printed in Hong Kong
9 8 7 6 5 4 3 2 1

Contents

In the Way of Thanks

Experienced and well-known writers usually call this part of a book "acknowledgments." Being neither experienced nor well known, I owe more than that to the many who gave of their time and knowledge. I owe them all deep and abiding gratitude:

My mother, Esther Miller, whose maternal and therefore biased pride and conviction that I could do anything I set my mind to, convinced me to try. She was my unflagging support who put up with hours of study, long absences, and the multitude of animals I brought home.

My father, Alexander Miller, who taught me that aggression begets aggression, force begets resistance, and that reason and common sense are the better way.

My teacher, William E. Campbell: there are no words to express the thanks to him for his demand and insistence on hard work, for his patience, advice, and gentle tolerance of my questions, cries for help, and unrelenting hero worship.

Peggy Campbell: an uncompromising but always gentle critic, a constant booster of flagging spirits, and above all—my friend.

Dr. James A. Craig, VMD, MA, who taught me medical diagnosis, recognition of illness, physical care, and who did his best to fill my head with knowledge. A true friend and confidant as well as my companions' physician, he cared devotedly for all of them and compassionately saw me through the loss of many of my animals friends.

All the veterinarians who gave generously of their time, gave advice, who were always available when questions about their patients needed answers, who gave praise and approval, and on occasion, even took my advice...

Dr. J. Warren Hamersma, who was on call at all times when I was defeated by my computer, who was able to retrieve stuff I thought I lost, and who—sometimes despairing of my technophobia—never lost his patience with me.

My sister, Nava Magen, who volunteered to proofread the manuscript. Without her help, it would have been a mess.

Thanks also for the wealth of knowledge I've received from Dr. Ron Morein (who took the time to answer my questions, no matter how ridiculous), Konrad Lorenz, Niko Tinbergen, John Paul Scott, Donald R. Griffin, J. Konorsky, Gerald Durrell, Michael Fox, S. J. Harless, Patricia Gail Burnham, Douglas Kirk, Linda Goodman, and the late John Fisher.

In addition, thanks to Bob O'Sullivan—my patient, understanding, and long-suffering editor, who after arguments with me, always turns out to be right.

All the countless, wonderful pet owners who taught me and who allowed me to teach them, and who believed that I am good at what I do, and the many who remained close friends to this day.

And last—but most assuredly not least—the companion animals who also taught and learned, who are safely with their families today because their problems were alleviated and who understood that I was there to help. Each one of them is real, only their names and breeds have been changed to protect the not-so innocent.

C. Miriam Yarden
Long Beach, California

Foreword

My first pet was a small black and white crossbreed named Ficko with whom I cheerfully shared cheese rinds when I was four years old. It made no difference that the cheese rind was his property—he shared it with me as willingly as I shared my buttered bread with him. It was as perfect a relationship between a human and an animal as possible with two natural, honest, and openly loving beings—a dog and a child. After Ficko's demise there was a world war, growing up to do, school, and no parental encouragement to acquire a pet.

Finally, along came Rex, the small black and white (mostly) English Fox Terrier. Despite his total weight of eight pounds, Rex would take on any dog, the bigger the better. Of course, he usually drew the short end of the stick, but that never daunted him. He was also intelligent, loyal, and a most loving dog. When he departed this world the whole family mourned him deeply.

For the next few years, marriage, a move to the United States, and attending law school kept me busy. The birth of my daughter gave me all I needed. When she was eight I was presented with a two-year-old Golden Retriever/Puli, and our lives were never the same again. The first major change Taffy brought about was that the landlord gave me notice because he had a no-pet policy (that he neglected to mention earlier). His argument, which he believed to be the most compelling, was "what does a nice Jewish girl like you need with a non-kosher animal like a dog?" It was quite useless to try to convince him that Taffy was not acquired for food but for companionship. So Esther, my mother, Andy, my daughter, and Taffy and I moved to an apartment building where among 11 apartment dwellers, there also lived nine companion animals without any trouble or undue noise. The surroundings were kept immaculate by the responsible pet owners, and remarkably there was little damage.

The other changes were those that all animal owners are familiar with: regular walks, visits to the veterinarian, exchanging notes and anecdotes with other pet owners…but the most significant change was the enrichment Taffy brought into our lives. She became a friend and confidant to my daughter, a source of pleasure and pride to me, and a protector and heroine to my mother after she chased a burglar from the apartment during the night while we were asleep. Above all, Taffy became our teacher and educator in an until-then unsuspected area: the human-animal bond, the special relationship we develop with pets, and the innate logic and common sense of animals.

When Taffy was seven years old, I brought home a tiny puppy threatened with extinction. She was the female replica of Rex, and Taffy adopted her enthusiastically, patiently, and devotedly. There was no need to house-train Aurora, she never destroyed anything, she only barked when the doorbell rang. Taffy taught her everything she needed to know. Taffy also taught me about patience, devotion, and the gentle but uncompromising discipline only a bitch is capable of. This part of her teaching was of great value to me with my child because I learned from her that I could achieve more by turning my back on a tantrum than catering to it. It was she who taught me that a human mother and child needed time away from each other on occasion, just as a bitch withdraws from the puppy for her own rest, relaxation, and mental stability. Taffy never felt guilty about abandoning Aurora for a short period of time, and because of her, neither did I when I left my daughter to her own devices and took a half-hour off from mothering. Neither Aurora nor my daughter suffered emotional traumas, and in fact, it did all of us a world of good.

That was more than 30 years ago. The reason the chronology is pertinent is because dog training was not considered as important then—unless you had a show dog or were involved in competition. Thus Aurora, like her surrogate mother, Taffy, was completely untrained. They were of course, house-clean. They came and sat when requested to do so, but of leadership, control, and training they knew nothing. Neither did I. For this ignorance, Aurora paid with her life. She dashed out in the rain, became disoriented, and when I called her she simply went the other way into the path of a speeding car. One week later, after heroic attempts by her veterinarian, she was euthanized.

That was my first experience with the emotional depletion the loss of a beloved pet creates. First, I saw her go up in the air and land with a thud. Then came the rush to get her to the hospital and the denial that anything serious could be wrong because she was alert and perky the next day. The paralysis in the hindquarters would wear off, or so I thought. Then there were daily calls to a compassionate and patient man who tried his best, and finally having to face that fact that nothing more could be done. When it was over, I was assailed by guilt because the accident happened as a result of my carelessness. I was angry at her for being so foolish as to go the other way when I called rather than come to me. I saw her for weeks out of the corner of my eye. I heard her happy yips before I opened the front door. And finally, I almost drowned in the sorrow and the emptiness her death created. Again, my friend and teacher Taffy came to the rescue.

Aurora died in March. In August, her veterinarian presented me with a puppy. She was gray and white, short-haired, prick-eared, and ugly. Mostly she had enough skin for three puppies, let alone one. Because of her strangely wild and ungainly looks, I named her Circe after the mythological enchantress who boasted of great beauty. At the age of ten, Taffy again assumed the care and mothering of a new puppy. I was looking to have the identical relationship with her as I had with Aurora, and again I learned from companions that each relationship is unique, and it is a wonderful thing that this is so. Aurora left a legacy for Circe: I was never going to allow such a tragedy to happen again through my ignorance. It was during Circe's education that I discovered Aurora's legacy to me: the deep interest and great desire to work with people and their animals.

I've given you my own personal pet history to convey the point that all my companions have been (and still are) my teachers. This may sound odd to behaviorists, scientists, or researchers, but all the invaluable knowledge gained from experts is not enough unless it is augmented by our animal-teachers. I am fortunate to have learned parenting from Taffy, communication from Aurora, devotion to small creatures from Circe (who grew up to be exotic and beautiful), patience and stoicism from Nefer. I also learned the sadness of emotional illness from my Beagle, Pip, and the pleasure of canine humor from Sombra.

Much of what I have learned and am still learning I owe to my countless pupils and their owners. All are unforgettable. Some stand out, like Peaches the Lhasa Apso who bossed her Boxer "puppy" Butch. The fact that Butch was at least five times her size did not seem to occur to either of them. There were Amie and Bijou, the toy poodles of elegance, lineage, and lovable silli-ness. I could never forget Tyler and Amanda, and later Jessica, the three great Great Danes. Muffin the West Highland Terrier was smarter than her teacher. Kristy the Husky-mix still greets me with excitement after her grad-uation at least eight years ago. Brutus the Golden Retriever—a star pupil; Han Solo the Doberman; Thunder the Rottweiler; Brogan the Irish Wolfhound; Bambi the Chihuahua; Schone the magnificent German Shep-herd and her adopted son Gandolf the Golden Retriever; and Max the Boxer...the list is endless and wonderful and generous. Read on for a taste of all these colorful characters and more!

Also, the multitude of owner/partners have taught me the wonders of the human mind and heart, which is open to changing attitudes, compassion, understanding, and the willingness to transform master-slave situations into human-animal partnerships. They give me the chance to show them logic and common sense only to find when they try it that "By golly! It works!" They tell me that they never knew before how much companion animals could enrich their lives now that they are able to communicate with them and understand each other. These owners came to realize that punishment is not a teaching tool, that their dogs do not have to reflect their own vani-ties, and that their egos are not so fragile that they must be protected by a pet for self-assurance. They learn that kindness and a gentle touch do not make them less in control.

On the other hand, in my years working with humans and their pets I have come across more than a few cases of abuse and cruelty. With very rare exceptions, these were the results of ignorance, old-fashioned ideas of how a dog or cat should be handled, or simply bad advice. I am happy to say that I am always able to change such situations and the great pleasure of such success is immeasurable. Yet there are other forms of cruelty and misguided behavior that are baffling—not always *toward* animals but *involving* them.

The saddest are the cases where pets are used for what I call animal blackmail. This happens usually when a parent tries to achieve a certain behavior or attitude from a child. When the child fails, the parent gives the child an ultimatum: either he complies or the child's pet will be given away/taken to the pound/killed. This is out-and-out blackmail. It teaches the child nothing, and while it may achieve an immediate result (cleaning his room, getting off the telephone, running an errand, etc.), the constant threat to the pet is stressful for the child and the animal. It is cruel and a form of brutality toward both child and animal.

Pets are used as scapegoats, weapons, and instruments of retaliation between people. Not only is this a prelude to disaster for the animal, but the humans who resort to such methods of interaction are also losers.

As for the behavior problems of our dogs, I should like to quote my teacher, Bill Campbell: "Prevention is better than cure!" I would add that cure is better than frustration, stress, unwitting cruelty, and rejection of a pet when help is possible and available.

Hopefully, this anecdotal book will be both enjoyable and educational for you as you share your life with a dog, especially if you're experiencing behavioral problems. Remember, nobody's perfect—we all need a helping hand once in a while, and it takes an extremely keen eye to interpret the multitude of signals your pup may send throughout his or her life. Once in a while, you've got to sit back, look closely, and say "Hey pup, let's talk."

CHAPTER 1

If You're Considering Dog Ownership

Bob Smith walks every evening with his large, magnificent, and friendly German Shepherd. You stop to talk to him from time to time and he extols the virtues of Champ. Richard Adams just moved in the house up the block and he has the most gentle Great Dane you have ever seen. He also tells you what fantastic dogs Danes are. But last week when the Jamiesons moved across the street, they paraded the most adorable Miniature Poodle who has the intelligence—they swear—of a ten-year-old child and is a veritable wonder and delight.

Here are the first pitfalls you can easily encounter: just because the Murrays have a beautiful Great Pyrenees or the Joneses own the cutest Bichon Frise does not mean automatically that either of these breeds will suit your needs and lifestyle. I say needs and lifestyle advisedly, because animals do indeed fill a need and your lifestyle will change.

This is why some preplanning is of great help. Reading is good, but talking with owners of the various breeds you are considering is even better. Most owners are willing to extol the virtues of their pets, and many are honest enough to tell you the problems you may face. What must be remembered is that not everybody is a big dog person. Not everybody is a small dog person either. I have met large, powerful men who are perfectly happy with their small Terriers, Beagles, Pomeranians, or Yorkies. I also know tiny women who not only adore but also control and interact with their Irish Wolfhounds, Mastiffs, or Great Danes in a way that is a pleasure to behold. So, once you have read, asked, observed, and pondered, you are ready to seek and find the right companion animal for yourself.

Finally you find Pupster, a dog that captures your fancy and your heart. What you must remember is that with very few exceptions, puppies are born perfect. The pet Pupster can easily grow into is what you make of him. With the proper education he will grow into as near a perfect dog as you could wish for. Without it, Pupster will grow into a perfect pest. You will end up the frustrated owner of a four-legged problem, overwhelmed by such impatience that may cause you to unwittingly inflict inhumane treatment on the animal you once envisioned as a loving member of your family, an important part of your life, and a source of pleasure and devoted companionship.

There are as many problem owners as there are problem pets. For the owner who refuses to grow with his pup, it would be better if he found a different home for his animal as a kindness to Pup instead of making him feel inadequate and insecure. It is true that the best motto is "an uneducated dog is an unhappy dog." But an uneducated owner is also unhappy and can lose control of the dog (and usually himself)—all preludes to the rejection of the pet. The pounds and animal shelters abound with such animals. So, I hope the experiences I share throughout this book will help you raise a happier, healthier, and more well-adjusted dog. I firmly believe that a well-cared-for dog will express the message "I love you, therefore I need you," rather than the other way around. This is an important distinction, and one of the main points of my practice.

Remember, whether your Pupster will be a source of joy and pleasure depends almost entirely on the demands you make on him and the expectations you have of him. Make your expectations unrealistic and you will create a problem. Demand merely human characteristics of him and you will be sorely disappointed. If you accept the premise that what you get out of Pupster depends entirely on what you put into him, if you believe that he is eager to please you, that a well-educated dog is a reflection of your leadership, care, responsibility, and affection, then you are embarking on one of the most satisfying experiences of your life. Above all, if you are prepared to commit about 12 to 14 years to a close and affectionate relationship, Pupster will repay you tenfold. He will enrich your life, alleviate your loneliness, relax you, amuse you, love you, and devote his life to you.

Basic Compatibility Chart

Before making a final decision on purchasing a dog, you'll need a general idea of the needs of your particular breed of choice. The chart below gives a *very basic* introduction to the needs of particular breeds. With a grade of "1" being the lowest, and "10" the highest, the chart covers the necessary grooming the dog will need, exercise required to keep him happy, suitability for city living, general energy level, and compatibility with small children.

Breed (Adult)	Grooming	Exercise	City Living	Energy Level	Children
Chihuahua	1	2	10	5	1
Yorkshire Terrier	10	2	10	8	1
Bichon Frise	10	5	10	7	3
Beagle	1	5	7	7	5
Poodle (small)	10	5	10	8	3
Jack Russell Terrier	1	10	8	10	4
Lhasa Apso	10	6	10	7	2
Dachshund	1	5	10	7	2
Dalmatian	1	10	2	8	5
Labrador Retriever	1	10	4	8	10
Golden Retriever	7	8	5	7	10
German Shorthaired Pointer	1	10	1	10	5
Weimaraner	1	10	1	10	5
German Shepherd	5	10	5	8	8
Greyhound	1	6	8	5	5
Rottweiler	2	10	8	8	8

- Please note that the breeds are *not* listed in order of preference but more by size.
- This chart refers to *adults,* not highly active, energetic puppies.
- Contrary to popular belief, Greyhounds require only one good run two–three times a week. They are affectionately referred to as the "85-lb couch potatoes."
- This chart does not take into consideration the temperament and disposition of each individual dog within the breed. However, small breeds are *not* recommended as companions for children who tend to view and handle them as toys.

CHAPTER

2

Puppy Comes Home

Y ou acquire Chester at the age of eight weeks, and he arrives home. You put him on the carpet and he promptly urinates on it. Problem? Not yet. This could have been easily avoided by not placing Chester on the carpet. Of course he will eliminate for several reasons. He just entered a new environment away from the security of his mother and lit-termates, he is bombarded with new odors, he cannot control his elimina-tory functions yet, and no one taught him that the carpet is not the right place for such activities.

Please, do not rub his nose into the mess! Not only is this cruel and disgusting, it is also quite useless as a teaching method. You also run the risk of com-municating to him that this is where you want him to do it—otherwise why would you emphasize the very spot in such a forceful manner? This mis-communication can start a habit of future wrong signals and misguidance of Chester.

Much has been written lately about the use of crates or cages in house-training. This idea is based on the theory that puppies do not soil their beds or nests. This is tantamount to expecting a human infant not to soil his dia-per because he will have to wear it! Puppies *do* soil their nests and beds—that is why their mothers ingest the waste in order to keep the area clean. Puppies would undoubtedly refrain from soiling their nests if they were able to. However, eliminatory control takes time to develop and proper habits have to be learned. A crate does not teach this, and too often the house-training problem is prolonged. When the soiling of the "nest" occurs and continues, the owner is perplexed because he was told that puppies don't do that. I do not approve of, nor do I use crates. Considering the multitude of problems a crate can create (self-mutilation, kennel syndrome, fears, exces-sive chewing, urinary problems), they are not good for puppy or owner.

Chester is now four months old and started teething. His mouth is sore and irritated, and the only activity that will soothe it is chewing anything he can get his mouth on. He is not fussy and does not discriminate between the old slipper you gave him or the $120 boots you left under your bed. Don't yank things out of his mouth and don't slap his muzzle, yell, swat, or employ other intricate and exotic forms of punishment. Teething is a painful business, and he will use any and all items to relieve the discomfort.

At eight months, Chester's teething is over, and he is reliably housetrained (he is, isn't he!?), but now he nips, snaps, and barks a lot. Don't toss him in the yard until he stops, because you can't teach a dog theory. He will not stop nipping and snapping and barking out in the yard. He will only learn to stop if you *teach* him to stop. He has no way of knowing that when you played tug-o-war with him, you actually taught him aggressive behavior, or when you allowed him to nip at your hand when he was a tiny puppy, you conveyed to him that this was a cute game. His mother or his siblings would never tolerate it. He doesn't know that his barking, which you used to say was the beginning of a great guard dog—and encouraged—is now annoying to you and your neighbors.

In other words, you cannot housetrain Chester in the backyard. It has to be done *inside* the house. You can't teach Chester to stay off the furniture unless you have the furniture there for him to stay away from. You can't expect Chester not to nip if you taught him that using his mouth was great fun, and you will never stop the barking unless you take the time and effort to teach him to discriminate between desirable barking and unacceptable, uncontrolled noise.

You may ask at this point: "How *do* I punish my dog for bad behavior?" The answer is "*Don't* punish your dog for being a dog." Don't punish Chester for the problems you helped create. He is not indulging in bad behavior; he is busy doing *unwanted* behavior. Instead, teach him good manners, socially acceptable behavior, and give him limits. He is willing and eager to learn, to please you and adapt to your home and life to the best of his ability. What does Chester ask in return? Not much: food, shelter, physical care, and emotional input from you. You would do as much for a child, right? Well, when you bring a puppy into your home, that is precisely what you are doing— bringing a new baby home.

Dogs in the wild have a society based on the pack and this pack has an intricate, rigid hierarchy. The best example is the wolf-pack, but feral dogs (household pets who have been abandoned) also form packs as an aid to survival. The strongest (mentally *or* physically) will step into the leader's place, and there will be a carefully graduated order of dominance and submission. When you introduced little Chester into your home and family, you in fact, allowed him to join a "pack," and his place in the pack must be clearly defined for him. Otherwise he will do his best to take the alpha-position and become the leader. This is natural for Chester. It is not natural for a human pack to permit it, and yet it happens too often. The dog's behavior, no matter how difficult or how much of a problem it becomes, dominates the life of the owner and he cannot cope with the situation. The dog is invariably the loser and sadly, too often rejected. Treat little Chester like a well-brought up child *after* you brought him up well. Never give him a command you can't or are not willing to follow through on. Even if you will not give that command again (until an hour from now or not until tomorrow), the one you gave must be complied with. This does not mean that you beat Chester into submission, but until he complies, do not let him leave the scene. Life with a dog is not a democracy. It is a benevolent dictatorship, with emphasis on benevolent.

In addition to the pack mentality and societal structure, Chester also has *become* a den-living animal. The dog you brought home, therefore, should also share the den with the new pack. Again, tossing Chester in the yard and not allowing him to become a full-fledged member of the pack will create more difficulties. Contrary to an ancient and still stubbornly held popular belief, there is no "yard dog" or "outdoor dog." There are only dogs who are kept in the yard and outdoors. Share your home as well as your heart, and again the rewards will far outweigh the small adjustments you may have to make.

It is hard sometimes to remember that though the six-month-old Great Dane, Gunther, may be as big as a house, nevertheless he is still a puppy. Don't expect adult behavior from Gunther because his body is huge. Give his brain time to catch up with his size.

A word about feeding Chester. Many people are under the impression that dogs are carnivores, but they're not. Dogs are omnivores, and a diet of pure meat without carbohydrates, fats, roughage, and all the other elements a mammal must have is unbalanced, unhealthy, and causes physical and behavioral problems. In the wild, canids and other predators eat meat, but they also eat what their prey has eaten, and in this manner, get the other foods and nutrients they require.

In the following chapters I shall touch on such subjects as housesoiling, destruction, aggression, fears, jealousy, loneliness, and so on. Each and every case has to be dealt with on an individual basis because *there are no textbook cases!* Each animal is as different, interesting, and fascinating as his owner. Dealing with their problems is not a matter of using a cookbook or a tried-and-true prescription of some sort, because no two situations are alike. The cause may be similar (as is the reaction), but the solution or management of the problem must be right for the individual human and animal in that wonderful partnership.

3

The Poop and Scoop Game

It is safe to say that there are almost as many causes of housesoiling as there are dog owners. The first episode the owner experiences is the one where Chester (remember him?) who just joined the household has not yet been educated in correct toilet habits. It is simple to housetrain a young animal, and since Chester began to learn at the age of about four weeks (from his mother and littermates), it is strongly advised that his education in this basic area be started the moment he enters the home. There are those who advocate waiting until the puppy is close to six months old, but I find it incredible that an owner would either live with the problem of cleaning up after the puppy for so long or, in frustration, toss Chester outside "until he is housebroken." Such an owner has never been able to explain to me satisfactorily, however, how Chester is supposed to become *house*trained without a *house* to be trained in.

There is a difference in the terms *housebreak* and *housetrain*. I avoid using the term *break* the dog in any way, regardless of the problem. The word *break* implies force, and I have found that by *educating* a dog, the owner achieves better, faster, and longer-lasting results.

Housesoiling in an adult animal occurs for many reasons. Moving a country dog to the city, or from a house with a yard into an apartment, is not only a major environmental and emotional change, but now he has no access to an outdoor toilet area. Chester is also not aware that the living room carpet is not a substitute for grass or cement. Many times housesoiling occurs because the owner moved into a house or apartment where there was a housesoiling dog and the carpets have not been properly cleaned. Chester smells it and hurries to put his own scent on top of the old odor.

Many dogs will mark territory, and this is a perfectly natural thing for them to do. The problem is that no matter how well you know the reason for this, and no matter how understanding you may be, the time will come when you will not wish to tolerate this activity no matter how natural it is. Urine is malodorous and the odor gets stronger as it sits in the carpet. It can also increase the aggressive tendencies in Chester—it is his territory, he marked it, and he will protect it. This is also natural and understandable for him to do. However, it is not acceptable in your home.

Housesoiling, which occurs after years of perfect toilet manners, is another matter. Whenever a client calls with this complaint, my first question is "Was Chester examined by his veterinarian for this?" If not, I suggest that this be done as soon as possible. There may be urinary system involvement, which the owner did not notice. There could be intestinal problems ranging from parasites to serious disorders that should be diagnosed and treated.

If Chester gets a clean bill of health, then we look for the emotional or environmental causes for the problem. Emotional causes can be jealousy, real or imagined neglect, not enough attention, too much attention, loneliness, fear, anger, or excitement, to name a few. Environmental factors can be as simple as not having access to the authorized area, placing the exit in a complicated spot, or having to negotiate a circuitous route to get to the right place.

Let us look at neglect, for instance. There was a time when Dad went to work and Mom stayed home to take care of the kids. For Mom, a dog was a welcome companion who never hollered "Mom, where are my clean socks?" or yelled down the stairs "Hon, there are no clean shirts in the drawer!" Fred the dog required little—food, shelter, medical attention; his emotional needs and exercise were more than well taken care of by the family as a whole. At night, Fred and the kids fell asleep tired and emotionally satisfied, secure and stable.

The above idyllic picture has changed. Nowadays, it is easy for everyone in the family to get caught up in a busy and active lifestyle. Perhaps Mom is now working at a career of her own, and the children's lives are also more complicated with extracurricular activities like sports, parties, or ballet. Fred still gets his shelter, food, and medical attention, but the emotional nurturing has diminished considerably. Even his grooming and baths are attended to by a professional groomer because Mom hasn't the time to clean up the bathroom as before, when Dad and the kids used to bathe Fred themselves. So one day, after Fred has been the perfect gentleman for years, he surprises everyone by urinating or defecating in the middle of the pale blue carpet in the living room—mostly when he is alone, but sometimes when his owners are looking on with horror.

The first reaction is a mixture of incredulity and anger. If the performance is repeated, the added ingredients will be frustration, a sense of betrayal on the part of the owner, and the belief that Fred is spiteful. There is also an overwhelming sense of helplessness in the face of such canine ingratitude for all the good things that have been lavished on Fred. Friends, relatives, neighbors, and various other people are consulted; 11 people will offer 15 different kinds of advice. All are tried to no avail. The results are more frustration and impatience on the part of the owners. And what about Fred? He is confused out of his mind! Finally, as an alternative to banishment the veterinarian is consulted. Hopefully he recommends a competent and experienced behavior specialist to consult with the family and offer help.

The above described behavior can also be triggered by the arrival of a new baby in the home, a new animal introduced into the household, a single owner gets married, a married couple separate, children go away to college, the wife takes a job (whereas until now she was at home), sudden increase of activity in the home (construction, renovation), decrease in attention, or even out of guilt—too much attention!

Let's get back to Chester. He is intelligent, and can be as manipulative and as inventive as humans. He can also be resourceful and very effective in the methods he utilizes to send his message. Can you think of anything more effective to get attention than leaving a pile of poop in the middle of the dining room? Is anything more dramatic than stepping into a puddle in the middle of the kitchen—with bare feet? Of course not! Your attention focuses immediately on Chester in wonder, anger, bewilderment, rage, and sympathy—all of them lovely ways of getting attention. True, not necessarily the good kind of attention, but Chester doesn't care what *kind* of attention he is getting. Attention is attention and some kind of attention is better than no attention.

When the behavior occurs for the first time, it is not yet a problem. It is a symptom that something is amiss. When the many different methods that have been gratuitously offered are tried—and fail—then it becomes a problem. Not only is the owner frustrated, but Chester is completely confused. The problem persists and probably will get worse. It certainly does not get better.

The most popular methods that are tried are a) dragging Chester to the evidence, usually hours after it happened, and showing it to him; b) pushing his nose into the mess; c) yelling at him; d) smacking him with hand or paper; e) having a heart-to-heart discussion with him; f) beating him to teach him a lesson; and g) tossing him outside and barring him from the house. Obviously such methods do not work, because if they did, I would not be there, listening to these sad stories.

The case of Cymbeline is a good example of unwitting neglect by the owner and the clear message the little Dachshund was sending.

CASE OF THE URINATING DACHSHUND

Cymbeline was a particularly small miniature Dachshund, spayed female aged nine months, and every part of her a true aristocrat. She was a little apprehensive of strangers, barked at them for a few seconds when they entered the home but settled into a friendly mood once they were inside and accepted by her owner.

Cymbeline's lady was away during the day at work and she had the company of the housekeeper and Spot, a gentlemanly Cockapoo who was the embodiment of good manners and friendly temperament. There was also the ten-year-old son of the house who belonged to Spot, as the lady belonged to Cymbeline.

While the pup was completely housetrained and used her doggy-door most efficiently, she developed a habit of urinating on her owner's bed and carpeting, at (to the owner) unpredictable times. She did this only in the lady's bedroom. It became clear that the owner's working hours increased and Cymbeline did not believe she was getting the attention she needed. She was sending a clear message that was misunderstood. She did not forget her housetraining, she did not develop a fear of the doggy-door, and she did not become lazy. She was signaling that she felt neglected.

It was recommended that the owner set aside a little time each day to spend exclusively with Cymbeline. This would be best achieved by taking Cymbeline into the bedroom when she came home from work and while changing into comfortable clothes and relaxing a little, close the door and talk to the pup, cuddle with her, toss her her favorite toys, and so on. It was crucial here that Cymbeline understood that this was *her* time with her owner—nothing and no one could encroach on it. I also recommended that the urination be completely ignored—unless caught in the act—and cleaned up in secret, out of Cymbeline's sight, thus sending a clear message that this method of attention getting will not work and she will not receive any for such unacceptable acts.

Within two weeks of following the above recommendations, Cymbeline stopped the indoor urination, resumed using her doggy-door, and the behavior did not resurface. An added advantage was that the owner thoroughly enjoyed the special time herself with her companion and found that it helped her relax when she arrived home from a strenuous job.

Cymbeline's sense of security and emotional stability have been so positively reinforced that when her lady left a month later for a week-long trip, Cymbeline did not have any accidents. To date, six years later, the urination in unauthorized places has not occurred again.

Drastic changes in a dog's life and routine can cause housesoiling problems. There are also times when the change appears so insignificant that we are not aware that the dog is disturbed. Many times there are several elements that contribute to the situation. Such was the case of Hermes who was unhappy (and overweight) and decided to take the most effective way to show his displeasure.

CASE OF THE TRADING COCKAPOO

Hermes, a ten-year-old neutered male Cockapoo was charming, good natured, and roly-poly. He lived in a small house without a yard, but his young owner took him out for walks three times daily for his toilet needs.

About five months before I met them, the owner bought a new sofa covered with a cream colored fabric. Having spent a considerable amount, she was devastated when Hermes began to urinate on it. She was convinced that he hated the sofa, since having been a perfect gentleman until then, why else would he use the sofa as his bathroom? After a thorough medical examination, which resulted in a clean bill of health, I went to visit the partners in this tragic tale.

When questioned, the young lady disclosed that Hermes was always allowed on the old sofa, but the new one was so handsome that she changed the rules. Not wishing to confuse him, she also barred all other furniture to him, whereas until the sofa came, he was allowed on everything. It was while she was at work that the crime was being committed.

Consultation covered not only this problem but details of Hermes' daily life, diet, exercise, and emotional environment. The little dog was almost 10 pounds (4.5 kg) overweight, his diet was not well balanced nor sufficiently nutritious, and Hermes was given no end of treats. When I met him he had trouble negotiating three steps into the living room.

First, we discussed diet and the urgent need for Hermes to lose some of his avoirdupois. He was put on a highly nutritious and balanced diet; instead of one meal a day, he was fed twice in controlled amounts and absolutely no tidbits. The walks now served not only as toilet relief but also a means to reduce his bulk.

Finally it was explained that since Hermes was always permitted on the furniture in the past, the new and sudden prohibition was a disturbing situation for him. For the life of him, he could not understand how this drastic change had come about and he was convinced that he was now unloved.

The owner suggested a compromise. We moved the furniture around just enough to place an older armchair by the window where the old sofa used to be. This was covered with a sheet and Hermes allowed on it whenever he felt like it as long as no one was using it. The longer walks, the loss of weight, and the two daily feedings reassured him of his owner's unfailing affection. The new sofa was, if not always ignored, never used as a bathroom again.

Within four days Hermes was happily enthroned is "his" chair, which the young lady decided to dedicate to him. He is much more lively and frisky now and his good health and condition belies his age.

Housesoiling is often the underlying cause for behavior problems that seem to build up like a pyramid. The owner only notices the most disturbing one and needs help in taking apart the structure he unwittingly created.

CASE OF THE MIXED-UP COCKER SPANIELS

Annie was a four-year-old, recently spayed female Cocker Spaniel who lived with her also recently neutered brother Jack. Skipper, a two-year-old neutered male, was their son. Mating, according to the owner, was accidental, and of the six pups Skipper was kept because he was the most timid. All appeared to be in good health. I was called in because the neighbors were complaining of constant barking when the owner was not at home.

During the fact-finding session I discovered that the owner had moved into his present condominium only three weeks before, from a house with a yard. His present patio was well fenced and he kept the little dogs there during the day while he was at work. Because of the close proximity of buildings and walls, the barking echoed and reverberated between them and the noise was considerable. On checking the patio, I found that the outside of the door was severely damaged by scratching and by teeth. When I asked the man why he kept them outside all day, he stated that they housesoiled and created a mess.

He was reminded that the three dogs had also just gone through a drastic change in their physical environment. In a strange and unfamiliar place, relegated outside, yelled at by irate neighbors, their feelings of insecurity were exacerbated. They clawed and chewed the door in an effort to get inside!

Here was a case of taking what seemed like "the easy way" out instead of addressing the housesoiling problem. Instead, not only did it prove to be difficult, it also created two additional problems: barking and destruction of the door.

It was not hard to refresh the dogs' memories as to the proper and authorized place for toilet functions. Once we installed a doggy-door, they used it happily and eagerly accepted the alternative. They now march out to the patio, eliminate and promptly re-enter without attacking the door and without barking to be let in.

I also recommended that the owner spend a little extra time with them every day to calm and reassure them in their new environment. He agreed to do so and began enjoying the special time with them.

This case clearly illustrates that symptoms can easily mislead us about a specific problem without realizing that it is the result of other events. In fact, the owner inadvertently created the barking by misreading the animals' message. The move was a circumstance he could not prevent, but it created an upheaval in all their lives. Locking them out in order to avoid the housesoiling created the barking and the destruction of the door. Had he addressed the housesoiling in the first place, the other two could well have been avoided, thus saving wear and tear on the nerves and unpleasant exchanges with the new neighbors.

As I always say to my clients once Puppy is housetrained: if your adult dog suddenly forgets his toilet manners, and he is found to be healthy, ask yourself "What have *I* done wrong?"

A word about punishment: Punishment is ineffective, especially *delayed* punishment. Chester does not remember that he defecated on the carpet as little as three *minutes* after the deed. How much less can he associate it with your anger *hours* later? Unless you can say to Chester that you are displeased *during* or *immediately after* the act, do nothing, or his confusion will be deep, which can easily turn into fear of you, making him into a "sneaky pooper" (eliminating behind sofas, chairs, and other hidden areas) or causing other forms of retaliation. It is his fear that will create what you perceive as acting guilty—not because he is aware of his guilt, but because he associates *your* words, *your* attitude, and *your* behavior upon finding the evidence, with the impending punishment.

CASES AGAINST CRATE TRAINING

Winston, a one-year-old neutered male English Bulldog has severe problems with closed doors: whenever he is accidentally shut in any room—even for a few minutes— he comes out like a raging maniac attacking anything and anyone in his way.

Kelly is a two-year-old spayed female Collie. She has yet to be housetrained. She has some fairly good perception of the requirement to defecate outside, but her urination is still erratic in spite of the fact that there are no medical or physical problems present.

A ten-month-old spayed female Pharaoh Hound named Kismet is terrified of open spaces and, having recently been adopted, refuses to leave a particular corner in the living room where she feels that she must touch both walls with her body in order to feel safe.

George is a two-year-old neutered male Labrador who has the kind of worn and damaged teeth one would expect to see in a geriatric dog, whose teeth have worn away due to age.

What do these animals have in common? They all have been crate trained. The training that was thus achieved is highly questionable, however, the side effects are not. They are quite evident and severe. In recent years, crate training has become fashionable because it is convenient for the owner. It also became lucrative for the manufacturers and sellers of crates.

The idea of crating a puppy is based on the mistaken premise that dogs are den-living animals and therefore: a) a puppy will not soil his nest; b) dogs like to be crated in their den; and c) it is a great problem solver. The facts are different. Dogs are *not* den-living animals! They live happily in *our* dens because we accustomed them to do so. If you observe canids in the wild, you will find that even wolves are *not* denning animals and the only time a den, cave, or sheltered digging is used is when the female gives birth. Once the cubs' eyes open and are weaned, they leave the den and join the pack in the open. To confirm this, call the Curator of Wolves at any zoo.

As for not soiling the nest, a puppy would undoubtedly not do so if he was able to refrain. However, until his sphincter control is fully developed, this is an unrealistic expectation. What he does learn, however, is that it is all right to eliminate where he lives! When he is allowed out of the crate and is expected to live with the owners, he has no idea that now he has to control himself, and housetraining becomes doubly difficult to achieve. In cases where the fastidious Baby Chester tries to hold his functions longer than he should, physical problems are often caused, not to mention the owners' consternation that this is a "dirty puppy" who is stubborn, or retarded, or spiteful.

The sad facts are that too many "crate experts" use the device to control the *symptom,* rather than work with the owner and the animal. Too often the owners are advised to leave the animal in the crate while they are at work for many hours, and Chester becomes cramped, inactive, bored out of his mind. He may try to chew his way out (and damage his teeth), or become terrified and fear any closed area or room. In human terms this equals claustrophobia. There are others who succumb to learned helplessness and the crate becomes their safe haven. The outside of the crate now becomes a place to fear. They will hug the wall and refuse to leave the area. The garden or yard becomes a place of terror. This is the equivalent of agoraphobia.

There are other side effects such as self-mutilation, small broken limbs (attempting to get out), stunted skeletal and muscular development, sluggish peristalsis due to physical inactivity, and deliberate retarding of mental development. Emotionally, these devices can be, and too often are, devastating.

One of the great joys in Chester's life is the frequent and delicious stretching. This tones the muscles, stretches the ligaments, awakens and stimulates the mind. Sure, the crate saves the sofa and the cushions, and keeps the waste off the floor, but it is a lazy, incompetent, and cruel way to deal with such problems. In short, it is a cop-out!

There are infinitely better ways to deal with problems than keeping Chester in tight, body- and mind-numbing solitary confinement. If indeed, the owner cannot be with Baby Chester every minute of the day, then a *restricted area* with the help of a baby gate is a far better solution. At least Chester can move about, play freely with toys, nap in comfort, and enjoy the lovely stretches he needs. He also learns the use of paper or pads as the first steps in housetraining.

If restriction is needed when the owner is at home, a playpen in the same room is ideal. Chester can't wander, he can still move about and the bonding with the visible presence of his owner is unhampered. A playpen will not cause claustrophobia, agoraphobia (cage syndrome), broken limbs, worn teeth, self-mutilation or the misguided message that it is OK to eliminate where he lives. The owner can easily lift him out and take him to his designated area.

With commitment and gentle, non-punitive work, Winston the Bulldog calmed considerably and when accidentally caught behind a closed door, he now barks politely to let his people know that he would appreciate being let out.

Kelly the Collie is learning proper eliminatory habits, albeit slowly. She will be reliable, but it is taking time.

Kismet the Pharaoh Hound is learning—also slowly—that the open space is not a place to fear. She still won't go out alone in spite of her doggy-door and will not stay outside by herself. At least she is going out. She started to sleep at the side of her owner's bed, but any stimuli she perceived to be threatening or frightening sent her back to the corner to hug the walls.

Crates have their uses in train travel, car travel (if the pup is not educated to stay calmly in the back of the car) and of course, flying. But crate training? No, this is not *training* in any sense of the word. It is merely convenient for the owner.

Teach Your Pup Good Toilet Manners the Natural Way

When you bring Pupster home, take him immediately to the specified area where you want him to eliminate. More than likely he will, because of the excitement of a new environment. This is the best way to show him his special area from the very start. Put him down and wait. Do not talk to him or play with him. This is not playtime—this is serious business! Wait until he eliminates.

Now walk to what he did, crouch down, point to it and praise what he produced with a happy "Good puppy! Clever puppy!" Pupster will approach to see and sniff what you are pointing at. At this time, give him a happy little chest rub. This is to teach him to associate function + location = praise. Now take him inside.

Teaching him where *not* to go is also pretty easy. When you catch him in the act of eliminating, do *not* punish him. You can, however, give him a firm tongue-lashing, using expressions like "shame," "disgraceful," "disgusting." Then take him out to his place, wait, point, and praise. Now leave him there long enough for you to come back to clean the accident *in secret,* and then bring him inside. Do *not* push his nose near or into the mess, do *not* swat him, do *not* throw him out to punish . . . remember, he performed an eminently *natural* function. Punish him, and you can easily create a sneaky pooper who goes behind furniture and remote corners because, while he knows you are angry, he has absolutely no idea why. Besides, within seconds he forgets that he eliminated and your anger is quite futile.

If you find an accident but did *not* catch him in the act, IGNORE it. Yes, ignore it! Walk past it as if it didn't exist and, *without any show of anger*, put him outside, sneak back, and again clean it up in secret. Pupster should *never see you cleaning up after him* because he perceives it as getting attention. He may also get the misguided idea that you like doing it and he will happily oblige by leaving other "presents." This is the poop-and-scoop game: he poops and you scoop. Once you have cleaned up, let him in as if nothing has happened.

Attach a small bell to his collar, so you'll know where he is. This is a much better alternative to *following him around all day*—that will make you nervous and tired and make Pupster nervous, frustrated, and spoiled rotten.

It's important that everyone in your home follows this training method. Spotty or erratic teaching will only prolong the agony.

Above all, please be realistic in your expectations of a young pup. After all, he has to adjust to you and your home. He is eager and willing to learn, but he will make mistakes. Try to accept them with understanding, patience, compassion, and a sense of humor.

And *please* remember, your puppy's best friend is a doggy-door.

The Realm of Our Fear

Aggressive dogs are frightening. I don't know of anyone who is unafraid of an aggressive dog (including myself), and with good reason! Dogs have at least two advantages that make humans vulnerable: powerful jaws with teeth designed to puncture and tear, and lightning speed. Many breeds have also the advantage of size coupled with power. Dogs can kill and have killed other animals and people. Not long ago, the dog was an untamed predator who survived by hunting and killing his food. The dog adapted better than any other predator to domestication. However, given the provocation or forced into certain circumstances, Chester still has the advantages that, when combined with his need for defense-attack, can result in tragedy.

Aggression has many faces, some overt, like rigidity of body, posture, tail position, ears, eyes, and mouth. It is also shown in vocalization, sometimes so subtly that we barely notice it. The most common aggressions that a pet owner will encounter are territorial, sexual, maternal, fearful, and over-protective aggressions. In addition, in multi-pet households dogs can fight over food, attention, the sofa, or the owner's lap. Some aggression is pain-induced due to injury, illness, or a physical condition of which the owner is not aware. The saddest kind of aggression is the type caused by the owner, since with some education it could have been avoided. Whatever the reason for the aggression, it often culminates in a painful injury whether to another animal or to a human. Naturally, that's when I'm called in for a consultation. So the following examples may clue you in to the causes of canine aggression so you can do your best to prevent it.

IMPORTANT NOTE

Sometimes a dog's behavior is seen as aggressive when in fact, it is not. Several cases follow of misread territorial, sexual, and other kinds of behavior. While these behaviors should be understood and sympathized with, remember that each must be handled because the ensuing injury can be serious and painful regardless of the motive behind it.

WHEN AGGRESSION IS DEFENSIVE

Sometimes canine aggression is defensive, and why not? Would we not defend ourselves as strongly and as aggressively as possible under attack or the threat of it? Devon had every right to try and defend himself. He just didn't know when to stop.

CASE OF THE GROUCHY CORGI

Devon was a four-year-old Corgi who came to his family at the age of nine weeks. About a year after his arrival, a baby was born, and Devon took it upon himself to be the infant's champion and best friend. He was, in every way, a delightful and beloved family member. Approximately six months before I saw him, he started to growl and snap at the husband and other men. He had not growled or snapped at the little boy or the mother—so far.

When I met Devon, I saw a beautiful little Pembroke (tailless) Corgi, well cared for and in excellent physical condition. Because of the initial interview on the telephone, I proceeded into the home completely ignoring his presence. In fact, I did not acknowledge his existence until he approached me and pushed his muzzle into my hand, much to the family's amusement.

On questioning the owners about themselves and Devon, I was told that about the time this aggressive behavior started, they had houseguests—the husband's brother and his two preteen boys. The guests showed no patience or understanding toward the dog and the children were caught several times harassing him.

One evening Devon was asleep under the table—his usual place—when the husband's brother felt him there with his foot. He bent down and for some perverse reason and without warning, yanked Devon out by his rump (remember, no tail!) and tossed him across the room. The fright and the pain to Devon had to be considerable.

A dreadful family argument ensued and resulted in the guests leaving early the next morning. Devon was not only scared out of his wits, his derriere smarting from the uncalled-for attack, but he also witnessed an emotionally charged quarrel, which added to his fright. A few days after the guests left, his behavior began to change to skittishness. He was now easily startled and the growling and snapping began.

Devon's owners attempted to remedy the situation by trying to soothe him, calm him, cajole him, and "love him out of it," not realizing that they were inadvertently *rewarding* his behavior. Within a very short time Devon realized that he could easily take over the leader's position in his pack by simply continuing the behavior that resulted in so much attention and reward.

By the time I saw Devon he had a good thing going and he was not about to give it up!

Just one recommendation was made. Devon was to be totally ignored, with the only exception being the caring for his basic needs—food and toilet necessities. If any attention or affection was to be given, it had to be initiated *by him.* He had to make the approach and the approach *had to be friendly.* At that time, he was to be given a simple command such as *sit* and on compliance, praised and given a brief but happy chest rub. Again, he was to be ignored until the next time he requested attention.

The family, while skeptical, remembered that when coming into the house, I ignored him. They also remembered that he showed interest, friendliness, and curiosity toward me and never growled or snapped. This helped me to convince them to give the method a try. The recommendation was strictly followed. Within ten days the defensive-aggressive display toned down considerably. Three weeks later the owners reported that they had their good-natured and sweet-tempered Corgi back again. He is still an excellent alarm-giver, which is essential, but the hostility and threatening aspects are gone and never surfaced again.

An interesting footnote: the brother and his children have been barred from the home. While it is not my place to recommend barring anyone from an owner's home, I agree in this case. It is desirable that relatives and friends not only accept the presence of a well-behaved and much loved companion animal in the home they visit, but that his place in the home and within the owner's family is respected. Barring anyone from a home is the right and the privilege of the owner. In this case, if the choice was between assuming the risk that Devon would eventually transfer the aggressive behavior to the small child, or barring people who are capable of gross insensitivity and harming the pet, then the choice is obvious to the owner.

A word about the method of demanding a simple act by the dog in return for attention and affection is important because it is used frequently and mentioned a lot in this book.

This method is called the "learn-to-earn" and it was devised, originated and named by William E. Campbell (*Problem Behavior in Dogs*, First Edition, American Veterinary Publications, Inc., 1975). Bill Campbell also called the maneuver "there is no free lunch." Since its inception, this method helped solve one of the most difficult problems, namely leadership. As mentioned before, it is not abnormal for Chester to take over leadership of the pack in many inventive, often unpleasant, and sometimes dangerous ways. He can do this as a young puppy or at any time later in life.

It is a deceptively simple exercise. We simply take Chester off puppy welfare! No free lunch! He will get no petting, no stroking, no fondling, and no affection, not even attention, *unless he earns it first* with a simple command such as a *good sit!* Once Chester complies with the request (please don't yell!), he gets an enthusiastic, brief chest rub, a *good dog!,* and allowed to go on his way. As many times as attention or affection is requested, this learn-to-earn will be repeated. And it must be done by *everyone* in the family, otherwise Chester will only interact with the one who makes no demands on him.

This simple exercise establishes, transfers, or reverts (as the case may demand) leadership to where it should be—with the owner. If Chester learned it as a puppy, chances are that he may not need reminders later in life. Should he get ideas of testing his limits, resuming the learn-to-earn will refresh his memory within a very short time.

I have seen mature dogs who were never put on this program before, respond to it, and after a few days of surprise, bewilderment, and some sulking, understand that there is a new order in their lives that is not bad at all. After all, why not *sit* when it brings praise, approval, and a good little chest rub?

AGGRESSION PROVOKED BY PAIN

Pain, whether caused accidentally or deliberately, can evoke an aggressive-defensive response. Put yourself in the dog's place and think of what you would do if someone thoughtlessly hurt you—and you had no way of avoiding such a person? Wouldn't you hit back, or at least threaten to do so? Well, that's what Coolidge did, and he was almost branded as aggressive by his owners who began to fear him.

CASE OF THE HURTING HOUND

Coolidge was a two-year-old neutered male Greyhound whose owners called for a consultation because from time to time he would growl at them. A few days before the call, he injured the husband's hand. The young man was concerned because as he stated "I do not wish to live with a dog I have to be afraid of." This is a reasonable attitude. I was curious to see why Coolidge behaved as he did.

When I arrived I found a remarkably beautiful, well cared for, extremely large dog. He was a little cautious when I entered but gave me his trust as soon as he led me inside and almost never left me while I was there. During the fact-finding phase I discovered that Coolidge had a habit of taking naps under coffee tables, end tables, behind the owners' bed, and other out-of-the-way places. When called, if he did not respond to the *come* command or feared a tin can filled with pennies thrown at him, the husband would pull him out by his front, or more often by his hind legs. That's when Coolidge growled! As for the injury to the husband's hand, it occurred when he again attempted to pull the large dog from behind the bed, and by his own account, it was more of a case of getting snagged on a tooth rather than an actual bite. As for Coolidge's reaction to the tin can, it badly startled the animal, heightening his reluctance to come when called.

We discussed Coolidge's "denning" behavior, namely that there are times when he wishes to be out of the traffic, have a quiet nap, and he needs occasional solitude and peace. He then transforms a piece of furniture into a safe haven. There is nothing wrong or unusual about such behavior—just as humans need solitude and quiet at times, so do animals. Once we understand this need, it is not difficult to respect it and allow Coolidge his space.

As for not responding to their call, it was simply a matter of the dog being startled and intensely disliking the noisy can that landed near him. I heard the sound and it was jarring to me, too. Instead, we worked on the effective way to give the *come* command. Not surprisingly, Coolidge responded cheerfully.

Because of his size and rolling gait it was strongly suggested that Coolidge be examined by his veterinarian for possible dysplasia or arthritis. He had never been checked for such possible disorders and no X-rays were ever taken. Apart from the fact that it is most unpleasant for a dog to be pulled or dragged by his limbs, the presence of such conditions as dysplasia or arthritis can be extremely painful to the animal. Two days later Coolidge had a thorough examination complete with X-rays. In spite of his youth, arthritis was indeed present and medical treatment was started. The owners now understood his occasional need for seclusion and respected his need for space and privacy. They call him correctly, and only rarely does he fail to respond with alacrity, usually if he is in deep sleep—then it takes him a few seconds. No growling has occurred and no more accidents with snagging teeth.

ORAL AGGRESSION

Outright nipping and biting is easily taught to a dog. When Baby Chester arrives in the home, he investigates everything with his mouth, like a human infant or toddler. This is the time when the new owner or the children decide that tug-o-war is a great game *because Baby Chester loves it.* Pet shops sell special rubber "tuggies" for this purpose. In no time at all, Chester nips and snaps at everything that moves and offers a resistance (including the owner's hands and ankles). Not only was Chester oriented and focused on his mouth, he was unwittingly taught aggressive behavior. He learned where his power is!

What now? What happens when you are not at home to continue the wonderful game of tug-o-war? Does Baby Chester understand that he has to wait until you get home to resume the game? Or will he continue to play the game by himself, with the drapes, the sofa, the pillows, the carpet, the books, the table leg—just about anything he can get hold of? You know the answer to that! When you come home, he wants to play the game with you, but you don't feel like it, or haven't the time, or are appalled by the damage he did, but you can't explain that to Chester. Instead, he will go for the hand that taught him the game and grab it in an effort to play. These are the beginnings of nippers, snappers, and eventual biters. And you, the poor owners, are upset, disappointed, and probably scratched and scraped, not realizing that it was all your fault.

Semiramis learned this behavior and never gave up the game until her owners despaired and were at a loss. Fortunately they called for help and she, being a most sensible lady, learned to stop this unwelcome habit.

CASE OF THE MOUTHY AKITA

Any orally oriented dog is a problem, but an Akita presents particularly serious implications. These magnificent animals are extremely powerful, intelligent, strong-willed, and can be single-minded in everything they do. So, when Semiramis never grew out of the habit of stealing an interesting variety of objects (tea towels, shoes, pillows, clothing, books) and refused to give them up without a good romp of tugging and pulling (and snarling and growling), the fun became a problem.

Sure enough, tug-o-war was Semiramis' favorite game and as a puppy her owner acquiesced readily and joined in the fun. Only now Semiramis was fully grown, wanted to play all the time, and if refused, she would steal the objects and bring them to "show-and-pull." The results were predictable: damaged articles, irritation of the owner, and Semiramis' confusion in the face of his anger.

This dog had to be taught that this form of play was no longer acceptable. Thus, whenever she took something in her mouth, she was to be given the command *good sit,* praised if she complied, and offered a toy in exchange. Each time she relinquished an unauthorized item, she was praised again, and I used the words "thank you!" as she let go. Soon Semiramis decided to test this new idea: she repaired to the bedroom and brought out a sock. She came, sat on *good sit!* got her chin stroked, and a toy was offered. She made the exchange to a resounding "thank you" and was rewarded with a brief and happy chest rub.

The owner was impressed with this "miracle." I emphasized that this was not a miracle and that no cure had been effected. A method had been introduced to teach Semiramis a different form of play: give up the towel/sock/shoe in exchange for something you like, perform a simple function *good sit!,* and be rewarded. I also emphasized that Semiramis must earn her praise and interaction with her owner by always responding to a simple command before she receives any affection or any stroking (learn-to-earn). In this manner, she will accept her owner as the leader and learn who is in charge.

The recommendations were followed and in about five weeks, Semiramis would try to present her owner with an occasional sock or similar now-forbidden object, but on the command of *good sit,* a soft stroke under the chin, and the words "thank you," she would be reminded that it was time to comply with her leader's request—"let it go!"

Semiramis now has a large array of toys, chewies, nylon bones, and so on. The last time I saw her, she took her own property in her mouth and when I called out "Semiramis, thank you!" I'll be darned if she didn't trot up to me, and with a grin on her face, deposit it gently in my lap!

SEXUAL AGGRESSION

Sexual aggression is as strong as the sex drive, and that's pretty strong! I'll never forget the man who came out of his house and caught his Great Dane Joe in the act of mating with his neighbor's willing female. In either ignorance or a state of temporary insanity (or both), he proceeded to grab Joe's collar and literally tore him away from the female. When Joe turned and went for the offending arm, mauling it severely, his owner delivered him to the veterinarian and in his outrage, demanded that Joe be euthanized immediately as a dangerous, savage, and vicious beast who "forgot his training."

Here was a man who was not only incredibly insensitive but also totally ignorant of the physiology of canine copulation and the genital structure of dogs. Once the mating tie has been established, it takes time for the release to take place. Thus, there was not only the frustration of being interfered with but extreme pain was also inflicted on the hapless Joe. Besides, no self-respecting dog will interrupt the mating process once it has started *merely to obey a command!* (I will not even try to extrapolate this to human behavior.)

Fortunately, the veterinarian was able to persuade the owner to allow the dog to live and the Dane was adopted into an intelligent, understanding, and knowledgeable family. No aggression of any kind was ever displayed again. It is also true that no cruel insensitivities were ever practiced against Joe either.

CASE OF THE AGGRESSIVE AIREDALE

Casey was a one-and-a-half-year-old intact male Airedale who, according to his owners, exhibited aggressive tendencies toward other dogs and toward the family's eight-year-old daughter, but never toward the twelve-year-old son. The call came after Casey got into a donnybrook with a Golden Retriever in training class. There was little damage done since another owner helped separate the dogs by lifting tails. It was interesting that the trainer in charge of the class offered no help at all.

Having heard the details (thinking that I heard everything), I asked if Casey had ever done anything like this before. The answer was negative. My suggestion was to have Casey neutered as soon as possible, and the family veterinarian gladly performed the surgery. About three weeks later I visited the family.

It seemed that Casey liked training class and never attempted to fight with any of his classmates before. Reviewing what occurred, it seemed that when I brought up the subject, the wife remembered that a new pupil was in class on the day of the fight, a little Sheltie female whose owner mentioned that she "had her little heat." The Golden Retriever was placed in class between the Sheltie and Casey.

No one would explain why a bitch in estrus was permitted to attend a training class that included unaltered males. Also, a presumably knowledgeable trainer was unable or unwilling to assist and advise when the fight broke out or after it was halted. In addition, Casey still appeared to be aggressive toward dogs on the street and persisted in biting the ankle of the eight-year-old child.

When I visited the home, I found Casey to be friendly, well-controlled, affectionate, and particularly fond of the child he was nipping—curious! He was a laughing dog who would grin at the slightest provocation and thoroughly enjoyed the fun and delight he gave.

I had to convince the husband of the innocence of this great dog and make him realize the stupidity and irresponsibility of the trainer who allowed a bitch in heat to attend her class. This not only risks but practically insures a fight between the males present. (We found out later that after Casey was removed from the class, three more fights erupted and many of the owners never returned.)

As for the aggression toward other dogs, this was suspect because Casey shared his home with two aging cats who were not too agile and as fun loving as they were in their youth. Casey never harassed them or bothered them aggressively. If he got a bit too rough with them, the cats would make a dignified exit. They were not afraid of the dog even though they had no front claws to enforce their sovereignty and long tenure.

We took to the streets in the hope that we would meet another dog so that the owners could demonstrate to me Casey's attempts to attack other animals. We were walking with Casey on the leash when a lady jogger came by with her dog, also on leash. We asked her to jog by us, and as soon as Casey saw the other dog, I gave him the *sit-stay* command. If he as much as attempted to move, I repeated the command, keeping eye contact with him. He held his position perfectly, calmly and quietly. When the jogger and her dog were at some distance, I released him (but kept him on leash!), praised him highly for his performance, and resumed the walk. Casey was not aggressive—Casey was friendly! He was a gregarious, social animal who wanted nothing but to make friends with everybody! Casey also wanted to play with everybody.

The owners were taught how to use Casey's training and obedience commands to repeat such performance in the future and if "aggressive" displays toward other animals surfaced again. Casey also made a lot of friends in the neighborhood.

Finally, his nipping and biting the child was dealt with. It was handled last, not because of presumed unimportance, but because heavy emphasis was going to be placed on this detail. Upon questioning the children, an entirely different picture emerged. Casey was not biting the child's feet because he was aggressive. He was pushing at her feet when he wanted to engage her attention. When the youngster did not wish to be bothered, she would *kick* his head, often connecting with his shoulder, face, and side. Casey, believing this to be playful, would respond with nipping the flailing foot and would occasionally connect with the ankles. To date, no injury had happened besides a few scratches, but unless the situation improved, injury was a distinct possibility, with the dog paying a heavy price.

I strongly emphasized that such behavior on the part of children is extremely dangerous, not to mention unkind. The kicking feet could hurt the dog painfully in the eye, muzzle, or ear, or Casey could get tired of such treatment. If he should retaliate for the sudden pain or frustration, he would inflict injury on the offending feet. At that time the child, having learned nothing, could develop a lifetime fear of dogs. Also a grave injustice would be committed against Casey.

Although my function is not to advise parents of how to bring up their children, I was there, indeed, to advise on the interaction and dynamics of the animal-human partnership. Such conduct on the child's part had to stop immediately. She had to be educated in no uncertain terms for the sake of her own safety. As I suspected, the parents were not completely aware of the sequence of events. They thought the dog bit the feet and only then the feet kicked out, instead of the other way around. Many a good animal has paid with his or her life because of lax parental supervision and lack of clear guidelines given to children on how to live intelligently, humanely, and *safely* with a pet.

Last, it was strongly advised that if discipline was deemed necessary with the child, it should not be done in Casey's presence. The child's activity and the reprimand were closely connected and if Casey witnessed the parental interference, there was a chance that he would perform the "correction" himself in the parents' absence—not a safe setup.

All the recommendations were followed with excellent results. Casey has not had a fight. The child stopped her aggression toward Casey and a close rapport developed between them. His performance on the street is exemplary and his family thoroughly enjoys the young fellow. His occasional theft of a paper napkin shredded to small slivers is willingly forgiven.

INHERITING ANGER

Aggression is an inherited trait. This is one of the reasons why it is essential that when you buy, choose, adopt, or are given a puppy, you meet both parents in person, hands on. Do not blindly accept the seller's assurances that both parents are "AKC, purebred, of aristocratic lineage, champion stock," and so on. All the registration means (despite the elegant family tree) is that the puppy was born. In other words, it is a birth certificate, which tells you *nothing* of the line's temperament, disposition, and nature. If you cannot meet the parents, walk the other way and find another breeder and another pup. In the long run—unless you have an expert test and evaluate the litter—you will be better off, and so will your dog.

While aggression *is* an inherited trait, it can also be created. It can be done by brutal handling where, if the dog's spirit is not broken, aggression will result. Yuki's case brought home to me that there are millions of people and hundreds of trainers whose idea of a good dog is one who has been mastered by his owner. He must know who is boss!

Personally, I fail to see the desirability of *mastering* a dog. Obviously, it can be done. A dog can be manhandled, even beaten into submission both physically and emotionally, but the result is not satisfactory. The dog should know who is boss, but this should be established intelligently, expertly, and with a light touch, without hurting or frightening the animal.

CASE OF THE VICIOUS HUSKY PUP

Yuki ("snow" in Japanese) was a fourteen-week-old intact female Husky who was acquired by her owners in a supermarket parking lot where she was being given away with her siblings, "free to good home," by an irresponsible person who failed to alter his pet. Yuki was selected by her present owner because she was a female and not as "hyper" as the rest of the litter. Of course, the litter could have been hungry, thirsty, tired, and excited, more than actually "hyper." This is not a good way to choose a puppy, and Yuki's owners were luckier in the long run than they realized.

When Yuki was fourteen weeks old, it was decided that she needed some training. She was promising to be large and had the potential to be a dominant personality who could easily take the position of the leader in the family.

When I went to the home, a pretty and well-cared-for animal met me who seemed well socialized. She had a laughing face and a friendly tongue and led the way inside the house with a gaily waving tail. The owners disclosed that they had seen a well-known local trainer before contacting me, who came to the house, put a choke chain around Yuki's neck, and proceeded to jerk her around so savagely that she spent the entire time with him yelping and crying. This left her with a fear of the leash, of course. They were also

advised by this person that they should get rid of her because the pup's reluctance to settle down during this "treatment" pointed to a potentially vicious and dangerous "streak." Fortunately they were sufficiently fond of Yuki and intelligent enough to seek a second opinion, and their veterinarian recommended that they call me.

Having spent a little over an hour with the family and Yuki, I came to the conclusion that she didn't have a vicious bone in her body. She had a great desire to be loved and petted and have body contact with her people. She also developed the bad habit of jumping on them, but no one knew how to convey to her that this was unacceptable. The other problem was that she was beginning to exhibit an excellent potential for guarding (not common in Huskies) and growled at the housekeeper whenever she came home from her day off, although she was very fond of the lady and willingly spent her days in the housekeeper's company.

We started Yuki's education with basic obedience and she proved to be singularly receptive and retentive. The only things Yuki did not know was what she had not yet learned. Once taught, everything remained with her for good. No leash, choke chain, or collar was used to educate Yuki. Her housetraining was set once she learned to use her doggy-door. She progressed through her teething with minimum damage to her surroundings. While she had to make considerable adjustment to her family and home, her owners were willing to adapt to her, once Yuki's emotional needs were discussed with them. In six weeks Yuki was a model of good behavior, sociability, and sweet temper. She was easily controlled by simple voice commands and walked on a leash without pulling—no mean feat for a Husky who is bred for the purpose of pulling! Not once did she exhibit vicious propensities, and to this day both the owners and I still wonder why she was so pronounced by a presumably knowledgeable trainer.

As for snarling and threatening the housekeeper, we realized that Yuki was used to seeing her in uniform. She came back from her day off in "civvies." Yuki simply did not recognize her and went a little overboard in her protectiveness. This was solved simply by advising the housekeeper to wear a light cologne at all times, but always the same scent. Thus, the problem completely disappeared when Yuki recognized the odor, regardless of the clothing the lady was wearing. In a relatively short time the scent could be dispensed with and the housekeeper came and went without any display of tension by Yuki.

To this day, Yuki is calm and good natured. She is also one of my favorites whom I visit from time to time because her owners remained my friends. She is affectionate even with her veterinarian—except when her ears are in need of treatment. She is highly sensitive in that area, but her doctor is aware of this and if problems are present, he handles Yuki with her feelings in mind.

MATERNAL, TERRITORIAL, AND HUMAN-CAUSED AGGRESSION

Maternal aggression is natural, inevitable, and necessary. I sympathize with it. The trouble is that too many people fail to make allowances for it, respect it, and understand it. Instead, they insist on encroaching upon it. Hence the protectiveness becomes more aggressive—as it does with any animal, including the human.

It is so much fun though, to show off the new litter and handle the tiny creatures, too often without regard for the mother's instincts and fears. It is essential for the mother to feel and act protectively toward her offspring— even aggressively—when she perceives them as being threatened. I learned my lesson well when I approached a new mother less thoughtfully than I should have (many years ago) and was warned by a resounding roar to back off, which I did. The owner was highly apologetic, but I explained that the fault was mine and I should be more concerned if the mother did *not* display normal maternal feelings.

Then there is the human-caused aggression, or aggression contributed to or triggered by the owner. The following case was sad because his owner was ignorant of the mental and emotional state of his dog. By the owner's account, Precious was brutalized by a well-known trainer in his area as a puppy, neutered for the wrong reasons, manhandled by his owner, allowed to assume the alpha-position in the family, and teased by the youngster in the family. In fact, just about anything that could have been done badly, was done badly.

CASE OF THE BITING ST. BERNARD

Precious was a three-year-old neutered male St. Bernard acquired at eight weeks of age by a husband, wife, and fifteen-year-old daughter. He came from a breeder in another part of the state, and they did not visit the litter. Having asked for a large and assertive male puppy, the breeder shipped them Precious.

The pup adapted well to the family and their elderly cat. At the age of seven months he was neutered at their veterinarian's advice because he started growling while his food was being prepared. He was also subjected to a particularly brutal form of training, which was discontinued, albeit too late, because the family could not stand the rough treatment their pet was getting.

About six months before I met the dog the first biting incident occurred. Precious, for all his size, slept on his owners' bed. He would leave the bed during the night, spend some time in the daughter's room, then in the hallway where he could keep his eyes on both bedrooms and thus alternate his sleeping places.

On the night in question, the husband was tired and irritable and ordered Precious off the bed. Precious refused to move and the owner tried to pull him off by his collar. Precious growled in response and the husband decided to "have it out with him." He put the choke chain around the dog's neck and jerked him off the bed, trying to slam him against the wall "to teach him a lesson." Why not? That's what the trainer did! Except that this treatment *by the owner* came as a complete surprise.

As it turned out, the lesson was learned by the man. The dog, in his fright, lashed out and punctured his arm in several places. After the incident, Precious became extremely subdued. Now another confrontation occurred between husband, wife, and daughter with accompanying yelling and screaming, the gist of which was that the husband got what he deserved.

Precious continued to be his usual sweet self for about six months. Then while he was dozing in the hallway, the daughter, on her way to another room, stepped over him. Startled at something looming over him, Precious reached up and grabbed the girl's wrist for a few seconds, leaving several scratches. No stitches were required, but their doctor suggested that they contact me immediately.

The family consisted of three people who were deeply involved emotionally with Precious and were understandably concerned about these "attacks." The dog met me in the front yard and after a few sniffs, led me into the house. He was a large, powerful, and handsome animal, slightly overweight, fed once daily. He was also an extremely dominant and bossy dog. He was protective of his family and fiercely possessive of them. They certainly did get the assertive and strong puppy they asked for, who now got all the attention he demanded, usually presenting his rump for a good scratch. When Precious was asleep, he would startle easily when waked by touch.

The worst times for Precious were early mornings and late nights when he seemed a little stiff and grouchy as he got to his feet. This prompted me to suggest that a medical examination would be in order, with X-rays of the skeletal structure, because I suspected that either dysplasia or a touch of arthritis might be present.

As for the biting incident with the husband, not much explanation was needed. He understood the mistake he made and the attack he directed toward Precious. The dog's retaliation was accepted by him as justified, and he never frightened the dog again. As for the daughter: I had a conversation with her and explained that her stepping over him was a mistake—some dogs are not at ease with such practices by humans. This is an extremely dominant stance and Precious did not accept it. He did not "turn on her" but lashed out at what he perceived as a threat.

The whole family got involved in the discussion, and I began to see the problem. One blamed the other, the other blamed the third, each had a better way of doing things, each had a different opinion with the argument getting hotter and louder. Precious sat in the middle, looking from one to the other, getting more and more tense. The only one who relaxed in the room was the feline senior citizen perched on the piano, laughing his head off.

After I asked for a chance to speak, they calmed down and we consulted together regarding their disagreements and varied methods of dealing with each other and with Precious. I explained that such arguments and loud discussions stress the dog and add to their difficulties. At the same time, for all their varied opinions, they all behaved submissively with him. This was explained in detail. When Precious wanted to be fed, they fed him. When he wanted to go out, they took him out. When he wanted to be scratched on the rump, they complied.

Once you've allowed him to take the alpha-position I explained, you can't expect him to give it up amiably. When you start a relationship with an animal as social and pack-oriented as a dog, it has to be under *your* leadership. This is essential for the family's peace of mind and the dog's emotional stability. However, if you make the mistake of allowing the situation to develop as it did with Precious, it *can* be turned around. It requires a careful, well-considered commitment on everyone's part. It cannot be done on a superficial, hit-or-miss basis, because the last thing you need, on top of all your existing problems, is confusion. Not only Precious' rehabilitation was at stake but the family's safety as well.

Recommendations were not complicated: wake Precious by voice, not by touch. Do not step over him. Feed him twice daily instead of once and get the excess weight off. Daily obedience sessions must be practiced—learn-to-earn for praise and petting—and do not scratch the rump! While working on obedience exercises, walk with Precious on the left, make left turns so that he is on the inside of the turn, which places you in the dominant position.

We set an appointment for a follow-up ten days later. Six days later I got a call: Precious nailed the daughter, not as painfully as the first time but again "without any provocation." I arrived at the home the same afternoon to hear what happened.

Precious was examined a few days before and hip dysplasia was found. His diet was modified to reduce the excess weight. It was advised by the veterinarian that certain activities be curtailed (jumping off high places, catching frisbees). Walking was suggested instead of the high-level activities. Three days before this last incident, the family was in the mountains for the weekend with Precious. It would appear that he thoroughly enjoyed himself, running, chasing, jumping—all the things they were warned against. Yet they allowed it because "he didn't seem to be in pain." They returned the same evening. Precious was finishing his dinner when the daughter called him over to give him a treat. She held it over his head and commanded Precious *Up!* He reared up on his hind legs, gave a thunderous growl, and got her wrist. The youngster was deeply hurt by Precious "betrayal."

It is not easy to tell people kindly that they are foolish, insensitive, and thoughtless. A painful condition had been diagnosed by their doctor. Precious' emotional needs were explained in detail. Their own emotional involvement was discussed and recognized. They were warned not to allow the kind of physical activity they not only permitted but also encouraged. Precious was on a slightly reduced food intake and yet the daughter not only teased him with a treat, she also demanded the physical performance that they were warned about. The fact that Precious did not wince, cry, or limp did not mean that he was pain-free, or that the rearing up did not cause pain. He did not wince, cry, or limp before either. Yet everything they were told and advised about by both the veterinarian and myself was disregarded. Unfortunately, this family left the state very soon after this incident and I was not able to conclude Precious' rehabilitation satisfactorily.

AGGRESSION STEMMING FROM PROTECTIVENESS

 A dog who is protective of his owner is highly desirable, but when the protectivness becomes exaggerated it can become a risky and dangerous matter. I'm not talking about the trained attack dog (that carries with it a calculated risk and I discourage it in the family situation). I'm talking about inadvertently created monsters. This is not hard to accomplish; it usually starts by rewarding Puppy Chester when he yaps at strangers. Soon the vocalizing develops into barking or nipping and from there the step to a bite is an easy one. Chester will grow up to continue this behavior and will become an uncontrollable peril.

A factor in creating such a dog is the owner's own fear and insecurity, which he literally *teaches* to the dog. Unfamiliar implements or objects in the hands of a stranger can present an impending threat (long poles, brooms, briefcases). My own Aurora consistently, valiantly, and diligently attacked the ironing board. She interposed all of her twelve pounds between it and myself, complete with piloerection, barking heroically at the board whether it was standing up or leaning against the wall, and insisted on protecting me from this terrible monster. Aurora came to me at the age of eight weeks and was never threatened with anything, let alone ironing boards, yet she perceived it as a threat to my safety.

Bossy, leader-type dogs can easily turn into overzealous protectors. Dogs who are constantly petted, fondled, and given indiscriminate tidbits learn quickly the rewards of such behavior. Without being aware of it, the owner actually reinforces the aggression. Two results can easily emerge: one, Chester, in an effort to please becomes increasingly more aggressive; and two, at any time that he wants attention or a goodie, all he has to do is show aggression so that the owner should reward him for stopping. Not possible, you say? Ask the owner of such dogs about the beginning development and the progression of this kind of behavior. They'll confirm it!

CASE OF THE PROTECTIVE NEWFOUNDLAND

Mirage was a two-year-old intact female Newfoundland living in a remote area of Southern California with a husband, wife, and a teenage daughter. There was also Lance, a one-year-old intact male Newfoundland who was Mirage's faithful friend and subordinate. Consultation was requested when Mirage began to show signs of excessive protectiveness toward her owners—against all strangers and visitors—something she had never done before. This activity began about six weeks before the call.

When she started this behavior, several changes had occurred in the family's lives. First, Mirage was flown to Montana to be bred but the mating was not successful and pregnancy did not result. Mirage was then flown home, arriving tense and tired. A few days later, the family left on a motor home vacation to another state, taking Mirage along. During the trip the wife experienced some anxiety in remote areas they visited, and she relied on Mirage's presence and size as a deterrent to strangers. Upon returning from this trip, extensive remodeling of their home started and for months on end workmen were going in and out, carrying lumber, tools, and various contraptions, making noise and causing the kind of upheaval and chaos such work entails. In a very short time Mirage was growling and snapping at non-family members. When she finally attempted to separate one of the workmen from his genitals, the family realized that help was urgently needed.

When I met Mirage she warned me, but I had her owner stand *beside* me rather than facing me and asked her to put her arm across my shoulder. We ignored Mirage and carried on a lively and jolly conversation, smiling and laughing, until she realized that her owner was relaxed, unafraid, and regarded me as a friend. Once Mirage calmed down, I picked up her ball and started tossing it to her, praising her highly each time she brought it back. After a little while she settled with us, probably thinking that anyone willing to toss her ball can't be all bad. Still, she remained a bit watchful. Lance, on the other hand, was friendly, affectionate, and very confident.

We discussed the causes of overprotectiveness in dogs and they began to understand how they themselves contributed to the problem. Mirage was a bossy dog and this was unwittingly reinforced—even by Lance. She always demanded a great deal of petting and fondling. As a result, she was not so much protecting her owners but rather the *relationship* she had with them, resenting outside interference from anyone. When she started to protect so zealously, they felt a little flattered that she cared so much for them.

They now also realized that the dog went through a lot of stressful changes and situations in a relatively short time. Two unaccompanied flights, an unsuccessful mating attempt, a trip to unfamiliar places, the wife's fears, and instead of her quiet, familiar, and restful home, workmen milling about for months with the resulting chaos. She didn't have a chance to rest from one tension to the next. By attempting to "calm her and love her out of it," they merely reinforced the behavior, rewarding her for the aggressive displays. When the problem was exacerbated, they started putting her outside whenever visitors came to the home—more stress, caused by being isolated from the petting, fondling, and the very relationship she was trying to protect. No wonder she disliked every visitor—she now associated him or her with her own isolation!

The most important step in Mirage's cure was the need for a change in her owners' attitude and their understanding. They began to realize that unless she was relaxed and accepting non-family members, she would never be able to differentiate between friend and foe.

First, all petting and calming had to stop when she became hostile. No more loving her out of it. She was immediately put on the learn-to-earn program and slowly exposed to as many people as possible, with her owners remaining calm and relaxed, conveying to her a confident attitude. If she showed any anger, she was immediately put on a *sit-stay* command, with the owner standing *beside* the other person (not face to face) and exchanging a few friendly words. When Mirage held the *sit-stay*, she was released with a *free!* and given a quick and happy chest rub.

The next step was to give the visitors a ball and have them toss it for her and praise her for bringing it back. Since this was her favorite game, she figured out (as she did with me) that if they are willing to play, they can't be bad people.

Finally, the most important step was reclaiming leadership from Mirage. It would have been unrealistic to suggest to the family that their beloved pet should never be petted or stroked, but it was vitally important that the petting be done correctly. Again, the learn-to-earn was emphasized, and all petting and stroking were stopped *unless* she performed a simple command first.

While this is simple to do, it is hard to remember because when we live with a dog, petting and stroking becomes an unconscious habit. We do it not only for the dog but also for our own satisfaction. To sit and watch television or carry on a conversation while your hand strokes and pets the soft coat of a dog can be pure pleasure. The dog loves it, too! If you stop, she will very often ask for more, and you comply. The day comes however, when the "ask" becomes a "demand," and if you don't comply, the animal has ways of enforcing the demand, as Mirage so ably demonstrated. Therefore, she was now never stroked or petted unless she performed a *sit*, a *down*, or a *stay*—whichever was appropriate at the moment.

In approximately six weeks of effort, attention, and commitment to turning Mirage and the owners around, leadership was back where it belonged—with Mirage's *owners*. She was calm and relaxed, and learned correct protective behavior, controlling herself and accepting visitors calmly. There are still certain people and situations she does not like, but her owners reason that they don't necessarily like every single person they meet either. As long as Mirage wishes to keep her distance from such individuals, they manage the situation in a most satisfactory manner. When Mirage had her next estrus, I received a call for advice as to the wisdom of breeding her. My suggestion was to forego breeding at that time and wait until the next receptive phase. Let her be relaxed, confident, and self-assured, and above all, don't ship her off to a breeder but bring the sire to her. This advice was also followed, and about a year later, Mirage became the proud mother of a healthy and vigorous litter. And the father? Why, Lance, of course! A proud papa whose presence Mirage accepted and welcomed.

MISUNDERSTOOD PROTECTIVE BEHAVIOR

 There is misunderstood protective behavior. Dancer's case was not without an element of humor. This magnificent German Shepherd belonged to a couple who adopted him from a humane adoption agency. Not much was known about his background and the first year of his life, but the wife was knowledgeable about German Shepherds. Not so the husband who never had a dog, was dubious about the acquisition and uncomfortable with the large male. The call came from the

wife who said they needed help because Dancer would not permit her husband into their bedroom at night *if the wife was in bed first.* Then she said, "You may laugh now if you wish. I've been laughing ever since it started."

Her husband certainly did not think it was amusing! He was convinced that they had a vicious, overprotective dog on their hands. In fact, Dancer was not so much protective as ornery and knew that the husband was afraid of him. It is more than likely that his previous owners experienced the same problem, which is why he may have landed in the hands of the rescue group.

When I met the couple it was freely admitted by the husband that never having owned a large dog, he was a little afraid of Dancer. Thus, my immediate work was with the husband to help *him* develop understanding, leadership, and rapport with the dog. Dancer was put through the basic obedience program, the work done predominantly by the husband. Dancer's response and willingness to accept him became a great source of pleasure for him, his fear dissolved and a close friendship developed instead. Dancer never barred the bedroom door again but was more than satisfied to sleep on the floor, next to the bed, on the husband's side.

HEALTH-RELATED AGGRESSION

Health related aggression is distinctly different. It is caused by physical discomfort and pain. If you have ever stubbed your toe hard and danced around the room with tears in your eyes—in a rage—you'll understand.

Animals differ from us when they are sick. While we want nursing, care, commiseration and sympathy from others, animals prefer to be left alone. They withdraw to a quiet, isolated, and safe place. Withdrawal and inactivity saves strength to fight illness and disease, and lack of movement conserves body heat needed for healing. Chester will clearly send the message that he wishes to be left alone to deal with the ailment and expend the energy required for recuperation. *Do not believe for a moment that Chester doesn't feel pain as much and as acutely as humans do! He is merely less vocal and more gracious about it, unless of course, you step on his toe.* Disturb, startle, or aggravate Chester when he is not feeling well and he will warn you to stay away. Insist on bothering him and he will lash out to make an emphatic point. Such was the case of Sunray who almost lost her life because she dared growl at an unsupervised, abusive child.

CASE OF THE UNHAPPY GOLDEN RETRIEVER

Sunray was a seven-year-old spayed female Golden Retriever, small for her breed and very gentle. She belonged to the mother in the family and lived happily until the older of two children started to toddle and walk, and show interest in her. Life was a little more hectic for Sunray then, but she took it in stride, sometimes taking leave of the area where the child was if things got a little rough for her. The consultation was called for when Sunray growled and snapped at the now four-year-old girl. The injury to the child was fright only, but help was certainly needed.

When I met Sunray she came to greet me with a smiling face, wagging tail, and a happy tongue. I squatted down to her and she was looking for my hand to push her muzzle into. However, when the four-year-old girl came near her, she would seek sanctuary under a chair or behind a sofa. This was not a vicious or aggressive dog—she would rather avoid confrontation if possible. It was also interesting to note that Sunray did not seek to avoid the younger child, a two-year-old boy.

Upon questioning it was disclosed that the little girl had been rough with Sunray at times, pulling her ears and tail, hitting her in the face, and throwing herself on top of Sunray while she was sleeping, with a resounding "Good dog!" The nipping incident happened at just such a time. Sunray was quietly resting in a corner of the mother's bathroom—her own, special, cool place—when the child sought her out, threw herself on top of the sleeping dog and got herself nipped.

Before anything else, I recommended that Sunray be examined by her veterinarian. Even though she was startled and did not have an avenue of escape in this case, something about her indicated physical discomfort. She was found to be suffering from transient pancreatitis and immediately put on medication.

The second consultation was spent discussing the relationship between the family and Sunray as well as the parents and the children. Comparisons were drawn between the child's treatment of the dog and her younger brother's, and it was found that the parents would never permit her to treat the smaller child as she treated Sunray. Two questions arose: a) Is the older child taking out her sibling jealousy toward the younger one on Sunray?; and b) Why did the parents allow this kind of treatment to be meted out to the dog?

Doesn't Sunray have certain rights and privileges in the family—namely the rights *not* to be stressed, hurt, frightened, and harassed? It was pointed out that by nature, a well-bred Golden Retriever is one of the gentlest of dogs, extremely patient with children, and a great playmate. Sunray illustrated this by tolerating the abuses from the child until it got too intense and painful for her, and it must have been a lot! She could have caused serious injury but her innate good nature prevented this from happening, and she was well able to discern the difference between the treatment she received from the two children. Therefore, I recommended that they forget putting Sunray to sleep, which the husband was intending, and start educating the children immediately in how to live with a dog humanely, responsibly, and above all safely?

To dramatize my point with the child (who sat and listened with a smirk on her face), with her parents permission to demonstrate, I startled the girl as hard as I could by yelling "boo!" at her when she least expected it. After she landed from her six-foot jump in the air and turned to me, prepared to cry, I asked her how it felt. Of course it felt terrible! She was scared out of her wits and angry with me. Well, that's how Sunray felt when she was unkind to her. She was that frightened, that scared, and that angry. Did she blame the dog for what she did? The point was so well taken that she forgot to cry.

The children were carefully supervised from then on and no more incidents occurred. Sunray was given the respect, space, and privacy she needed when she was not up to playing, and the children are still learning valuable lessons in compassion, understanding, and humane treatment of all living beings.

AGGRESSION TOWARD OTHER ANIMALS

Dogs sometimes show aggression toward other animals. Not everyone is as fortunate as I was when I introduced two small kittens to my eight- and nine-year-old dogs, Circe and Nefer. Until then a cat was something to bark at if one dared enter the yard. Knowing how to introduce them contributes greatly to such success, and of course, if you don't tell dogs and cats that they are enemies, they'll never know. My dogs still snarl at free-roaming cats but they treat free-roaming dogs the same way. However, they do it from the safety of the front window and they bark at people also who walk past my house at times, in spite of our repeated discussions that the street is a public thoroughfare and people have the right to walk there. They remain heroic in their efforts to scare them away from behind the protection of a reinforced screen door or window. Konrad Lorenz describes this as "fence courage."

Alas, such hatred is too often encouraged and too often taught to dogs. Some people believe that it is cute, macho, clever, and desirable that their dogs chase cats, squirrels, and birds, and if they can, to catch and kill them. What they don't realize is that this deliberately reinforced prey-chasing behavior can, and does at times, develop into prey-chasing directed toward other creatures, like children, joggers, and cyclers—in fact, toward anything that runs or goes by.

Fights in multi-pet households are aggression if they are consistent and uncontrolled. Skirmishes, the setting of hierarchies, short food fights, and females snapping at amorous males are not desirable or fun but can be handled with patience, the understanding of what causes such rhubarbs, and the use of learn-to-earn. When the case is that of one dog persistently going after another, then steps must be taken or the animals permanently separated. This can be done in the home at the cost of serious environmental changes (one dog kept indoors while the other is relegated to the yard—not an ideal solution), or one of the dogs re-homed. This is a sad solution, especially when both dogs are loved, but it's better than constant bloody fights with accompanying injuries and sometimes death. What is left then, is a program of correcting the behavior of the aggressor, the victim, and above all, the owner.

CASE OF THE CAT-HATING DOBERMAN

About six months before the consultation an intact male Doberman was found on the street, lying in the grassy divider in a high traffic area. He was malnourished, so thin and weak that he had to be lifted into the car. This Dobie looked old, gaunt, listless with dry skin, dull coat, every bone showing in sharp relief, eyes swollen shut, ears infected, and had several old scars on his body.

The couple who found Marshmallow took him for a medical examination immediately. It was found that he had conjunctivitis, badly infected and undoubtedly painful ears, intestinal parasites, several neglected bite wounds, and a broken front tooth, as if he tried to chew his way out of some enclosure (chain link fence in some junk yard?). However, the molars were extremely clean and healthy.

The question was what to treat first. The eyes were cleaned and medicated, and so were the ears. Dewormed, he was given several gentle baths and a feeding regimen was started designed to help him regain the weight he lost, obviously to starvation. All through this, the Dobie was unique in his gentleness and sweet temper in the face of sometimes unpleasant medical treatment, and he seemed to display gratitude for all that was being tried in order to help him.

Marsh responded well to treatment. He was finally rid of the worms, the eyes were bright and clear, the ears were healed, the infected wounds were now bad memories and he began to fill out. Strong muscles began to ripple as he walked, he had a spring in his step, and he no longer looked old! He was shiny and sleek and obviously much younger than originally believed. After neutering it appeared that Marsh's problems were over in a loving home. Although one badly cropped ear never stood up, Marsh had a rakishly appealing look and his personality remained gentle. His devotion to his adoptive parents knew no bounds.

He had one flaw that might never have become a problem: he "hated" cats and his new home had an existing pet, a two-year-old neutered male cat who was trying to make friendly approaches to Marshmallow. It seemed however, that the dog had certainly been encouraged to chase cats. He would give Sebastian the cat a good chase and then look at his people as if expecting praise for the excellent job he did. His people had no intention of re-homing the cat or Marsh, so they sought help.

When I met Marsh for the first time, he was powerful, elegant, sleek, and self-assured. Having examined me thoroughly, he allowed me into the house, sat in front of me and lifted his paw. He also proceeded to show me how well he could chase Sebastian, who managed to elude him—again. This was also the first time that I heard Marshmallow's trials and tribulations, the efforts that were made not only to save him but to find his previous owners. That effort fortunately proved unsuccessful.

Rather than wait until the Dobie managed to catch the cat, help was needed right away. And since this cat-chasing behavior took time to develop, it could not be solved immediately. A program was therefore designed for this great dog, to be followed diligently and consistently.

We started by placing Marsh on a leash and having his owner hold it. We brought Sebastian into the room and Marsh immediately tried to go after him. However, he was held by his owner who was on the other end of the leash, which was not pulled, tugged or jerked—merely held. After a few minutes the cat was taken out of the room and Marsh given a few *sit* commands and praised upon compliance, with enthusiasm and general happy noises. This method was used for two weeks on a daily basis, until Marsh sat calmly in Sebastian's presence without having his leash held. He was still to be distracted every time he showed more than curiosity and friendly interest, given the command and again praised for his performance.

For the next two weeks the exercises were continued with the leash attached to Marsh's collar but not held. When he seemed to lose interest, we began to work without the leash. The program worked very well because now Sebastian would come to Marshmallow, who would gently nuzzle him and sniff the cat from stem to stern.

After six weeks of this education and corrective program, the owners were delighted to find Marshmallow one day, asleep on their bed with Sebastian curled up under his chin, also sleeping. The pets still play, and Marsh occasionally will give chase, but the nature of the play has changed. The dog is not serious, the cat is not frightened, and when the play is over they settle down to what they consider a well-earned nap in each other's arms.

FOOD-RELATED AGGRESSION

Food-related aggression (food protection) is dangerous, especially around children. Many trainers believe that if you repeatedly snatch Baby Chester's food away and then return it, he will accept such behavior on the part of humans. While it is essential that an emotionally stable Chester should be able to cope with some incidents of stress, *this is not one of them*. Such "training" has created many aggressive food-protecting adult dogs (starting this display around seven to eight months). This form of misguided training is actually *teasing* the puppy with one of the most important things in his life—his food. When he shows anger at such times, the owner is advised to punish the pup by shaking him, slapping his muzzle, yelling "NO!" into his face, and hard as it may be to believe, some "experts" even hang the pup by the neck.

This leaves Baby Chester with no reason to *trust* his owner in the face of such goings-on. The Grown Chester cannot trust the owners' children when they tease him in this cruel way. Of course, if he growls at one of the kids, he is punished even more severely and may even lose his life.

Whenever I consult with a client whose companion growled at a child who disturbed him while eating, the conversation goes something like:

"What would you do if you were hungry, sat down to a good meal, and someone kept snatching your plate away from you?"

"I would probably smack him silly!" is the usual reply.

"Would you allow someone to do this to your child?"

"No, I certainly would not!"

"Then why should Big Al permit it? Why should he not have the same respect and peace when *he* is having *his* dinner?"

"Oh! I see what you are saying. I guess you're right..."

So, a little understanding of why Big Al growled, some rules set down for the child (or restraint if she is too young for rules), or what I find even more desirable and safe—an isolated spot for Big Al to have his meal without interference manages such problems very well. What is even more important, the child learns a lesson in consideration and good manners, a sound basis for future humane and perceptive animal ownership.

Unfortunately too few owners call for help and too many good dogs are destroyed for this unwittingly created and much misunderstood aggressive behavior.

Food fights are not uncommon in multi-pet households, and dogs who have lived in harmony and peace for years will get into a donnybrook when one decides to investigate the bowl of the other. Distance is the answer here. Feed them as far from each other as possible and be ready to take control if necessary. This is a management problem.

CASE OF THE CAT-KILLING PIT BULL

Without a doubt, Eva was the biggest, most powerful, and fearsome looking Pit Bull I had ever met. Although her owner, a young engineer, reassured me that she was a loving puffball, I really had my doubts when I first met her. She was five years old, spayed, in excellent condition, and had lived with her owner since she was a nine-week-old puppy.

Eva turned out to be exactly the kind of loving puffball her owner claimed. Convinced she was a lap dog, she simply settled on me once I sat down. Not that I minded, but when my legs went numb, I had to invite her to get off. She was gentle, affectionate, and calm, but two weeks before she had begun to kill cats and her owner was justifiably concerned.

Eva indulged in one specific behavior her owner mentioned: she was a dedicated food guarder. Once her food was placed in her bowl and given to her, it was the better part of valor not to approach her until she finished. She protected her food with ferocity even from her owner. Since he lived alone, this was not a problem he chose to change; he preferred to just live with it. For five years of Eva's life it was never an issue.

The home was undergoing major renovation and remodelling. To keep Eva from being underfoot and stressed unduly while eating, for the past two weeks he had served Eva her meals outside on the patio. That is when the cat killings began. So far, no neighbors were searching for missing cats.

We discussed the nature of hungry stray cats who will come into yards to eat from dogs' dishes. Although the resident animal will often ignore this, permit it, or merely chase the cat away, there are those who take sterner measures with intruders. Eva was protective of her food to begin with, so not only did she not tolerate or permit this, but she carried the defense of her food to extremes by actually killing thieves.

We also discussed why feeding dogs outside is not smart. Eating should be a family affair (indoors), and the lack of cleanliness because of flies and bird droppings outside is a basic health hazard. Then there is scavenging, which can (as it did here) lead to extreme measures taken by the food's owner. Feeding outside also encourages visitors to enter the yard, driven by hunger and convenience, with tragic results when the guests are unwelcomed by the resident dog. This is precisely what Eva did—protected her food to the extreme.

Since the young man elected to manage Eva's problem rather than eliminate it (and this is always the privilege of the owner), not wishing to stress a five-year-old dog by "training it out of her," I strongly advised him to resume feeding her inside. Before concluding the consultation, we brought Eva's dish inside and showed her where it was. In order to let her withdraw from the work going on, a doggy-door was installed to enable her to retreat inside or outside to a quiet spot. Eva accompanied me to the door like a gracious hostess and with a final show of affection, let me leave.

Upon follow-up two weeks later, the young man reported that not a single cat had been killed. Although Eva still chased uninvited feline guests, she had a different attitude. Now she merely gave chase and an ultimatum as they went over the fence. No executions occurred again.

One year later, her behavior still did not revert back to killing, and word must have gotten around in the feline community of her neighborhood to avoid this particular yard.

INBRED AGGRESSION

 A word about inbred aggression. Not long ago I was called to consult with a couple on the aggressive behavior of their eleven-month-old Akbash. This breed is a very large, powerful sheep-guarding dog, a native of Turkey. He is sometimes called the Anatolian Sheepdog, and to date he is not too well known and, hopefully, not overbred. This is a hardworking dog who guards against wolves and other predators most admirably. They are also active, highly protective, and need lots of space to expend their excess energies. They are admirably suited for the work they have been bred to perform. However, the Akbash is not the greatest pet in the city. Highly territorial, bossy and physical, intelligent and able, he is also affectionate and possessive of his owner and his owner's property. These are the attributes that make him an excellent guard.

Transplant a dog like this into an urban backyard—even with an acre of space—and he will become bored, restless, and more possessive. He tends to overdo the job of protector here.

The dog I visited was all these things. He was handsome as they come and enormous for his age—more than 100 pounds (45 kg). He could only be brought into the house on a leash if there were visitors present, and his owners had difficulty restraining him (what would they do when he was fully grown?). He had bitten two people so far, and the wife was scared of him after he growled at her a few times.

They knew nothing about the breed when they fell in love with the four-month-old puppy who came bouncing up to them, bowling them over with what they perceived as affection. Although they knew that the ideal age to introduce a puppy to the human pack is between eight to nine weeks, they just loved him at first sight. Since then they had contacted other Akbash owners and all agreed with me—Akbash do not make good city pets.

There wasn't much I could do for them. They would not allow me to approach the dog for fear that I would be attacked. As for attitudes, they were interesting. When the threats by the dog started, the wife wisely began to put an emotional distance between herself and the dog. She knew that her fears would grow and the dog would not be able to stay with them. The husband, who spent considerably less time with him, wanted to keep him because he loved the dog. There were heated exchanges between husband and wife. It was difficult for her to convince him that she was truly fearful that she would not be able to control him.

They had an option: re-home him with a friend who kept sheep on his ten-acre property and was willing to the take the big pup. My suggestion was to let him go (such suggestions by me are rare) and let him do what he does best, what he was bred for. Let him utilize his energies and aggressively protective nature in a useful and constructive way, protecting the friend's herd of sheep.

IDIOPATHIC AGGRESSION

Finally, there is another kind of aggression, perhaps the most fearsome and dreaded: idiopathic. This word means the behavior is caused by an undiagnosed or undiagnosable physical condition. This can be brain damage, tumor, fluid, pressure, and so on, and the symptoms are usually unpredictability, varying time periods between episodes, and attacks on people the dog knows well and is used to, without provocation or cause. The attack is as fast as lightning, without warning (growl, snarl, curling lip, or show of teeth), and the injuries are severe. This is no love-nip! After the bite there is no show of regret, exhaustion, or withdrawal on the part of the dog that can be observed after a provoked or caused attack or a fear bite. The dog behaves as if nothing happened. He is not even aware that anything did happen! Idiopathic behavior usually surfaces at about the age of two to three years, and there are no early warning signs.

This kind of problem is sad because unless the condition can be alleviated medically, there is little hope that it will improve or go away. Training is little help because it is not a training problem. Most of the dogs I have seen with such idiopathic behavior were well trained as youngsters and did not forget their training. Sadly, the only recourse is euthanasia before the dog becomes life-threatening (big dogs, especially) and before the owner is facing a lawsuit, in which case the court can and often does demand the destruction of the dog.

A word about punishment: punishing for aggressive behavior is not only pointless but also dangerous. The dog is aggressive already and to have him face an aggressive human is an outright challenge. He will direct the aggression toward the one meting out the punishment (read "attack" from the dog's point of view). This is natural and predictable. If he is large enough, you will be badly hurt. If he is small, you can injure him in ratio to the rage you happen to be in, not only physically (many dogs have been treated for injuries inflicted by angry and then guilt-ridden owners) but psychologically as well.

There is a good rule that I have found works well: never punish physically when you are angry. Perhaps this works well because if you wait until your anger dissipates, you will avoid acting out of irrational rage and retaliation, and you will probably think of better ways to deal with the problem.

Finally, it is highly advisable to familiarize yourself with the body language of aggression in dogs. These signs include territorial urination, direct stare, erect ears, piloerection (hair standing up on neck and back), backward lean, "giving the eye," growling, and sharp barks. It is also wise to educate children on the subject of what to do when meeting an unknown, frightened, or aggressive dog.

CHAPTER

The Noise Makers

According to practically all city animal control agencies, barking dog complaints far outnumber all other calls they receive. Dogs have great stamina when they start barking and can go on for hours during day or night. They can get hoarse from barking for hours on end! Living in an apartment complex where a dog barks for eight hours while the owners are at work can be unnerving to say the least. A dog who barks all night in the yard is more than unnerving—he evokes hatred in those who are kept awake by the sound. In many areas laws are being enforced more strictly than before or new ones are being enacted to eliminate this most unwelcome nuisance.

Dogs bark. That is their language or "speech," their method of alarm-giving, greeting, complaining, and communicating with other dogs both near and far. My Circe used it to tattle on her housemates and called me to come and see the crimes they had committed. There are different keys and intensities to the bark: Terriers are yappy, Poodles sound sharp, Beagles howl, Huskies sing, and many others roar.

When barking becomes uncontrolled, constant, or remains unchecked, you have a problem. Problem barking carries with it additional difficulties, especially if your dog's duty is to alert you of strangers or unauthorized entry to your property. As a problem barker, Chester finds himself in the position of the boy who cried wolf. If he barks all the time at people, cats, dogs, falling leaves, and balmy breezes, how do *you* know which bark is the alarm or the warning? You can't take every sound he makes for a real alert, thus you have the tendency to ignore the noise because "there goes that dog again!" This is how you gain a problem and lose a potentially good protector.

The first, almost instinctive response by most people to a barking dog is to get his attention by a louder sound than he is making, or out-shout him. The trouble with this is that it is very difficult to do and the dog "shouts" back. You yell even louder, the dog "yells" back, and before you know it, you are in a barking match. Considering the stamina and staying power of the dog, you can guess who will lose this competition. In fact, you may be conveying to him that barking is a good thing. After all, you taught him to "speak" when he was a pup, and look how much you are enjoying it now.

You may stop a barking dog when you are around, but what about the time when he is alone? With determination and patience, even that can be halted. Let's look at the spot Basso found himself in.

CASE OF THE BARKING SCOTTY

Basso should never have been named that! His voice was as high pitched as any I have ever heard, with a capability to pierce eardrums. Never have I heard such a sharp, annoying bark as poor Basso's. The consultation took place as an alternative to de-barking the little fellow.

He was a sweet and affectionate Scottish Terrier, groomed to the hilt, in excellent condition. He was a foundling in the California desert and it was not known whether he was lost by his previous people or dumped by them. He wandered by the present owners' car when they stopped for rest. The pup was tired, starved, and thirsty, his coat matted with filth, and his paws were raw. When I met him he showed none of what he had been through and was an excellent companion but for the noise.

On observation I realized that this was a case of enthusiastic alarm-giving. This would have been fine, but then he got so carried away that he just didn't know how to stop. It was a matter of "now that I started, how do I quit?" Territorial, he was doing his best to alert his new family. His gratitude knew no bounds! Between the barking bouts he was delightful, tractable, and proud of his good looks.

While consulting on this situation, there was an opportunity for me to observe Basso's performance. Someone passed by the house under the living room window and Basso started his alarm-bark. It was done well, his timing was perfect, but he got carried away again. At this point the owners made the error of trying to "out-bark" Basso. They began shouting at him, hoping that if they were louder, he would stop to listen. No such luck! The barking match went on for a while until they gave up and I could distract Basso and focus him on me. Lovely silence was our reward.

Basso's motivation and performance were explained to his owners, and they saw that this problem was not a matter of bad behavior and not a case of their loss of control of Basso. It was a case of *never having had control* of Basso. They misunderstood what he was doing and instead of teaching him appropriate alarm-giving, they were trying to be the boss barkers themselves.

When the next stimulus occurred and Basso went into his act again, I demonstrated how to stop him calmly, without anger, impatience, or stress to themselves or to the fourteen-month-old pup. This consisted of *going to investigate* Basso's real or imagined reason for barking. Failure to do this has two results: a) Basso will not stop; and b) there may *be* an intruder about whom he *is* warning them. If his alert is checked out and respected, then acknowledged with a "well done" followed by a simple command of *sit* for which he is rewarded (remember? happy and brief chest rub?), they would have a truly fine watchdog who would soon develop the ability to judge the need for giving alarm. He would also learn to control himself so that the alarm-bark does not turn into hysteria.

The owners learned the method with little trouble and mastered the timing, patience, and persistence needed. They also learned to resist the urge to shout at the little dog. They learned that the more they lowered their voices, the more effort Basso made to listen. For the next two weeks they followed the recommendations faithfully. Each alarm was investigated (be it day or night), the silence followed with a "well done!" An immediate *sit* command was given and happy praise for performing it. Within the two weeks there was a marked improvement in Basso's barking habits, and within five weeks they could leave him alone at home for a few hours without complaints from the neighbors.

Basso is a responsible and reliable alarm-giver now. He was always a delightful companion, but now his pride knows no limits because of the constant, *well-earned* praise and appreciation he receives not only from his family but from the neighbors as well. His vocal cords remained intact.

There is no miracle involved in such a cure. It involves understanding the *reasons* for the barking, observing the trigger or stimulus, the location, the time, and the manner in which the barking is done. Then it is a matter of re-educating both the owner and the animal to understand what is required of them, what kind of barking is permitted, and how the undesirable kind is to be stopped immediately. While the adaptability and understanding of the animal is a wonder to behold, it is not so much miraculous as it is sensible and logical.

Holly's problem was a drastic physical and emotional change in her life. Not only did she have to get used to a new location, but the focus of her attention, affection, and emotional dependence disappeared and a new one had to be formed toward a new person, another dog, and an entirely different physical environment. As was described previously, if a dog finds herself called upon to defend a territory larger than she can comfortably handle, she will tend to be nervous and more aggressive in performing her job. Holly now had a large yard, new sounds, new sights, new scents, and new entities to get used to, and felt that it was more than she could protect efficiently. So she simply overdid the job she assigned to herself.

CASE OF THE HYSTERICAL POODLE

Holly was a four-year-old spayed female Miniature Poodle adopted by her new owner about a week before I met them. Her previous owner had owned

her since she was eight weeks old and she was the only parent Holly ever had. That lady had to enter a nursing home, and it was heartbreaking for both. Holly was fortunate to find a second, equally loving and caring home in a house instead of an apartment, and a new friend, Sasha, a two-year-old neutered male Random Breed who accepted her happily.

Holly's problem was that while she would bark reasonably at birds, bugs, and falling leaves, she would also get hysterical if she caught sight of the next door neighbor whose yard was separated from hers by a vertical, open slat fence.

Holly appeared to be in excellent physical condition (if a tad overweight). She played and ran enthusiastically with Sasha, learned to use the doggy door in no time, and both were sociable, friendly, and affectionate.

The yard was spacious, well-fenced, and ideally suited for exercise and recreation for the two little dogs. I inspected the fence between the two properties where the barking occurred and during this time, the neighbor came out into *his* yard. Holly saw him, took a firm stand and started barking sharply. It was a high-pitched Poodle bark and she really put her heart into it! It was a definite statement to the neighbor that he was seen and would be watched!

We returned to the house and discussed the situation. Sasha had been through obedience training, but Holly was an unknown quantity in this respect. Upon testing her it became evident that she, too, had some training—certainly enough for the owner to exercise a good degree of leadership with her. Thus it became easier to proceed with a program or re-education for both Holly and her new owner.

Considering the fact that she had been in her new home for only a week, her behavior was not hard to understand and sympathize with. An apartment dweller all her life, the yard was something to get used to, and because of its size she felt tense about guarding it. Since Sasha did not bark at the neighbor, she felt that he was not doing his job and took it upon herself to do double duty.

First, I suggested that the open slat fence be covered temporarily with a reed-type material so that Holly could not see the neighbor's movements on the other side. Second, daily obedience sessions were started lasting five to ten minutes both inside the house and in the yard. Third, since Holly's new owner was on friendly terms with the neighbor, I asked her to invite him over, introduce him to Holly and let them become friends. This way she gets used to his appearance, voice, and scent. When she next sees him in the yard and hears his voice, she will recognize him *as a friend*.

The rest of the barking was to be handled in a manner similar to the case of Basso, checking out the barking, giving Holly a "well done" and the command to *sit* and praise. In fact, Holly's owner was so adept in learning the program that she could distract Holly *before* she started unwanted barking. All recommendations were followed and with a little patience on the part of the neighbor, Holly was given more time to get used to her new surroundings and lifestyle. She calmed down within a reasonably short time and her barks toward the neighbor became greetings of brief duration followed by quiet. In four weeks time the reed covering could be removed from the fence, and peace returned to the two households.

Holly and Sasha still bark when the doorbell rings or they hear a knock on the door. I suggested that this habit should not be discouraged. For a woman living alone, this canine service is valuable.

The owners' emotional state and behavior directly affect the emotional state and behavior of their companion animals. Loud arguments and fights between husband and wife, or boyfriend and girlfriend, which the dog observes can create common and uncommon behavior problems. Two dogs in the same household may react in two different ways to the same situation, as did Kiko and Pika.

CASE OF THE HOWLING BASSET HOUND

Kiko's life was a pleasant one, all 18 months of it. A young couple shared their home with him and with Pika, a four-year-old spayed female of the same breed, who was his surrogate mother. They lived in a comfortable home in the San Fernando Valley. Kiko's health was excellent, the dogs' needs were cared for in every way, and all seemed well. Why then, did Kiko start howling two months before, whenever he was left in the yard with his friend Pika, and keep howling until his human came home from work? Had anything changed out in the yard? Did someone agitate him out there?

When his owner called for a consultation, she did so with some degree of embarrassment and doubt, because she had never heard of "animal psychiatrists." Also, she had dogs before and never experienced any problems with them. After she checked my references, we set up an appointment.

When I met Kiko, Pika, and their owner, I found out that no physical changes had taken place in the yard and no one had agitated the dogs out there, so the problem was not related to the yard. There was no change in the owner's routine or work hours in the last two months that could have accounted for the problem. However, there was a drastic change just before the howling started: the owners were divorced. It was not a quiet divorce and both dogs were present during many arguments and quarrels between the couple. When the husband moved out, it was a drastic emotional trauma for everyone. For Kiko, this change was unsettling, stressful, created insecurities, and he missed the husband.

Pika did not react the same way. She was happy and calm; she accepted the situation and was not unduly upset. Yet even her calm air could not reassure the little male. The neighbors began to worry and eventually complain about the unwelcome serenade that went on during the day.

As if all this were not enough, Kiko was reaching sexual maturity and repeatedly attempted to mount Pika. She, being spayed, was not interested in the least and rejected the amorous attempts, at first patiently and then with a growl and a shove when the youngster insisted. Kiko now began to masturbate on the sofas, pillows, carpets, towels, and everything he could get hold of. When I met him he was beginning to mount people, and while some of the wife's friends thought this was cute and funny, I explained that there was nothing cute or funny about it. On the contrary, it was sad because of the additional stress this created in the dog's life.

Several recommendations were made. First, neuter Kiko without delay to relieve him of a drive that could not be dealt with naturally because Pika was of no help to him. This recommendation was readily accepted when the details of the surgery were explained (it is astounding how many people are under the impression that neutering means the surgical removal of the *penis*!). Second, because Kiko never howled inside the house, a doggy-door was installed immediately and allowed the pair free access to both inside and outside. This is very reassuring to a dog because he knows that whichever side of the little door he is on, he can always get to the other side of it. Both dogs were reliably houstrained and never showed destructive tendencies, so the door would not cause any problems.

The wife was in the habit of getting up every night to let the dogs out to relieve themselves, thinking that they couldn't hold their urine "because in small dogs the bladders are also small." I explained that while it is true that in small dogs the internal organs are small, they are nevertheless the right size required for normal functioning. While a Basset Hound's bladder is smaller than that of a St. Bernard, he is well able to control the sphincter muscles and such nocturnal attendance is unnecessary. After all, they drink Basset amounts of water, not St. Bernard amounts. In the event that they feel the need to urinate during the night, the doggy-door and a small nightlight will serve very well to allow them access to the yard and back again. This arrangement will also allow her uninterrupted sleep.

A little structured playtime was suggested to convey to them (especially to Kiko) that the caring and love did not stop or disappear, that their lady was involved with them emotionally, that life hasn't changed all that much, and that both he and Pika are as important as before in spite of the husband's absence.

All the recommendations were followed. As suddenly as the howling started, it stopped. The wife could go to work, vary her schedule within reason and not worry about Kiko's howling. They now sleep through the night without interruptions and Kiko's amorous advances have abated. Pika is delighted about that! No damage was done inside the house, no accidental soiling, no chewing or destruction of any kind. As for animal psychiatry, the wife is now a believer and happily gives the best references I could hope for.

Too often owners labor under the misconception that all behavior problems will disappear once the dog has obedience training. Unfortunately, too many trainers perpetuate this myth and large amounts of money and time are spent on training that does not address the problem itself. I have seen dogs as well trained as any Marine continuing the activity that created the problem in the first place. When the training does not do the trick, the next trainer will suggest that more training is needed and the third and the fourth...I recall a nice little Bichon Frise whose training cost a total of $5000, paid to four different trainers. The little dog could have been a first-place winner in obedience, but he continued to howl and housesoil.

Dogs and Children

My good friend Douglas Kirk, a trainer, psychologist, and author in Canyon Lake, Texas, says that a child without a dog is like the sky without the blue. As a general statement, I heartily agree. Young children on the whole, with the open mind, imagination, and receptivity of youth, make excellent dog people. At the same time, whenever I am asked "What is the ideal age for a child to have a dog?" my answer is never definite. I don't believe there is an ideal age for a child to have a pet. I know youngsters as young as four or five who are gentle, compassionate, and considerate with their pets and who get better at it as they mature. I also know children of all ages whom I wouldn't trust with a stuffed Pound Puppy!

The animal-human partnership is an individual matter. Some people are excellent at it, some learn it, and some should not involve themselves with it. In the case of children, the addition of an animal to the family has to be conditional on pre-educating the child, supervision by the parents, and above all, the right breed. Unless such details are addressed, the addition of a dog can develop into a sometimes heartbreaking, sometimes dangerous situation, with the blame always placed on, and the ultimate price paid by, the dog. Sadly, too few parents are interested in *why* the dog nipped the youngster. All they know is that he did and the dog ends up trashed or dead.

Many calls come in from people seeking help in finding a good home for their companion animals of several years because of the impending birth of the first baby. They've heard too many horror stories of dogs attacking and tearing babies to pieces. The stories about the evil nature of cats with babies is even fancier. In the case of 99 percent of such calls I am able to change these owners' attitudes and work with them to achieve a happy and safe coexistence where neither the babies nor the dogs get hurt. The remaining one percent is so adamant in their misinformed decision that to change their minds would not only be futile but also dangerous. They don't realize that stories of attacks appear in the news *because* they are few and far between. Unfortunately, it is such news that creates the misconception that dogs injure or kill infants as a part of their nature.

Of course dogs have injured and even killed infants. However, if the two beings are properly introduced and both treated with common sense and *vigilance*, such tragedies can be avoided. Sometimes it is better to re-home a dog who is one of the few exceptions who does not take well to children. That is plain common sense!

While the best way to start a child-dog relationship is to bring the dog to the child instead of the child to the dog, this is not always possible. In innumerable cases, couples have had their family companions for a few years before the baby arrived, and there is no reason why the new child and the established dog should not live together in peace and harmony. As I said, we read the lurid headlines that somewhere a cherished family dog has injured or killed the new baby, and we shake our head in horror. The fact is that this could have been avoided with some preparation and effort.

The work has to start with the dog *before* the baby is born. The nursery should not be barred to Chester. He should become familiar with it and be comfortable in it. Let him see the new furniture, the new arrangements, and *let him smell the baby powder and baby cream.* If you bring the baby home and bar him from the room, he will want to get in there more than ever!

Make sure that Chester is free of external and internal parasites. Flea control and a simple fecal test will point the way to treatment. Today, with the new flea preventive products, there is no excuse to harbor such pests in the home. Eliminating worms is simple, inexpensive, and safe. Common sense bathing and brushing of the pet is highly recommended.

Four to five days before the baby is due, the mother-to-be should create a little emotional distance from the dog. This means that he receives a little less attention, less affection, and less involvement from the mother-to-be. Chester may be a little confused at first, but once the baby arrives, this will be remedied.

While the mother is still in the hospital, ask the nurse attending the baby to give the new father a small shirt or other garment the infant wore. This carries the baby's scent and when given to the dog, he will become familiar with the new smell he will be meeting soon. **NO DIAPERS, PLEASE!**

Some behaviorists suggest that before the birth, a baby *doll* be used for role playing with the dog. This seems somewhat strange because it imparts a kind of stupidity to a dog that he does not possess. A *doll* does not *smell* or *sound* like a human infant and the dog may chew it up *simply because it is a doll.* This does *not* mean that he will chew up the infant. Above all, it teaches Chester nothing. If the owner wishes to indulge in this exercise, fine, but I would not rely on it as an effective teaching method. After all, many dogs have stuffed animals such as puppies or cats for toys, yet they would not dream of chomping or chewing up a live puppy or kitten when confronted with one.

Off-leash obedience work is vital because it is diffcult to control a dog on a leash with a baby in one's arms. This is where heavy emphasis must be placed on the *sit, stay,* and *off* commands. This ought to be started when the dog is a puppy and kept up throughout his life. Refreshing his memory and skills is a good idea during the pregnancy. However, it is never too late, and I have worked successfully with many committed, expectant parents.

When the baby is brought home, the dog should meet the family outside. Let the father hold the baby and the mother should greet the dog with enthusiasm and a great show of affection. This is where the emotional distance is now closed and the attention withheld a few days ago is resumed, so that he associates it with the arrival of this new, strange looking and funny sounding creature.

Now go into the house, let the mother sit with the baby on her lap, and allow the dog—on a loose leash—to investigate, smell, and even lick the baby. This is important for recognition, acceptance, and the beginning of bonding with the child (the baby can always be cleaned with a washcloth, and if the dog is healthy, he will cause no harm). Now put the baby in the crib and give the dog a little more attention and affection. Allow him to investigate the child in the crib (which he cannot get into). *Common sense dictates that baby and dog are never left alone without supervision.* This is the moment when the sensible behavior on the part of the parents begins and will continue for the coming years. Remember that Chester has to get used to this little creature with the familiar scent but the unfamiliar, sometimes startling sound.

Those who succeed in such an introduction are those who do this calmly, quietly, and *without* a crowd around. Many people milling about is unsettling and exciting for the dog and he may become overactive. What he and the baby need is a calm and quiet time to deal with this change.

Do **not** exile the dog to the yard while nursing. Have him in a *sit-stay* or *down-stay* mode and praise him for performance. This will eliminate a feeling of exclusion. Also, try not to upset the dog's routine too much (of course, the baby's routine is important). With a little patience and inventiveness, routines can be adjusted or worked out in a matter of a few days.

Once the baby is six to eight months old, start *his* education. Take his open hand and stroke the dog saying to the baby "good doggie" or "good Chester." This does register and by the time the child toddles, this becomes second nature and the best insurance for all concerned.

We know the insecurity and jealousy that first-born children sometimes exhibit with the addition of a second child to the family circle. We understand it, sympathize with it, and do all the right things psychologists and child-experts advise to help the older child conquer such feelings. It does not occur to many people that a dog who has been living with a couple for several years as their "baby" will experience the same fear and feelings of insecurity when a new, strange "puppy" appears in the spare bedroom. He is fearful when his "parents" are remote from him physically and emotionally because of the funny-smelling and funny-sounding creature in the house. They have less time for him, he is not allowed to investigate and sniff the newcomer, he is yelled at a lot now—maybe even relegated to the yard, whereas before he had the run of the house and even slept in the bedroom. And the ultimate betrayal is that sometimes he even gets swatted or hit when he goes too near the baby—something that never happened to him before!

The dog gets nervous, tense, and resentful. He has been rejected in favor of the new baby. He may feel forgotten, ignored, emotionally abandoned. When he does manage to find the child unprotected, he could (and sometimes he does) retaliate exactly as he would against a new puppy who was incorrectly introduced to him. Please remember also that the cry of an infant reminds animals of the sound of wounded prey. If the prey-chasing instinct is strong, the dog will react. Therefore, *never* place a baby on the carpet and then leave him alone with the dog!

In the case of Whisky, the parents were neither able nor willing to make the effort required. They were too fearful of the very same dog they adored until the day the baby came. It didn't surprise me that a gentle, affectionate, beloved, and loyal companion suddenly took on the characteristics of an uncontrollable, vicious monster.

CASE OF THE BABY IN THE HOME I

Whisky was a handsome, neutered male Australian Shepherd. He was strong and powerful but friendly and amiable. For the first two years of his life he was the center of his owners' attention, living in the house and sleeping in their bedroom.

The newborn son was brought home at the age of four days. No effort of any kind was made to prepare Whisky, and when the baby and dog met, everything was done badly. There was a crowd of friends, neighbors, relatives, both sets of grandparents, uncles, aunts, and more. There was also a new nanny (who proved to be the most sensible of them all). The noise and excitement were considerable and Whisky joined in the melee, becoming excited himself.

When the baby was shown to him, he was held back securely by a choke chain, allowed to approach the baby, and immediately jerked back. He was alternately petted, yanked, stroked, slapped, pulled, admonished, and made about as nervous as possible. The crowd volunteered conflicting advice, and when Whisky somehow attempted to smell the baby, all hell broke loose. There were expressions of horror, anger, and consternation, and everyone was yelling at each other. Finally, poor Whisky snapped his jaws in the air (still held by the choke chain), more than likely trying to inform the people that he had had enough. He was then tossed outside and only permitted in the house when the nursery door was closed "to keep the germs away from the baby" and keep him safe from this bloodthirsty animal. If Whisky as much as sniffed the nursery door, the parents were convinced that he was "trying to get the baby."

During the consultation, they demonstrated to me that Whisky was "rough and hostile." When taken into the nursery, he was allowed to sniff the crib with the baby in it, but when he put his paws up and tried to see him, he was roughly jerked down by the husband's white knuckles again and again. At my suggestion their *demonstration* was stopped.

The owners' attitude, upon questioning, was admittedly one of fear, which seemed to be so overwhelming that they could not deal with it. They realized that the introduction was done very badly indeed, but by now their fear was too deep to work with their companion. Added to this fear was the suddenly developed concern over the "disease" he began to spread since the arrival of the baby. They proposed to relegate Whisky to the yard permanently.

My recommendation was against this because they would have to be constantly vigilant to make sure that the emotionally abandoned dog would not slip back into the house, and his frustration at this turn of events may be such that the baby could be endangered.

Because the parents were unable and unwilling to deal with their fear and work with their pet, it was recommended that a new home be found for Whisky. Fortunately this recommendation was followed and Whisky found a loving home with friends of the family.

CASE OF THE BABY IN THE HOME II

This is the story of Chateaubriand, a two-year-old neutered Great Dane whose owners called for assistance about a month after Whisky's sad tale. They requested advice *before* and eventual help for the time *when* the baby came home. Several steps were suggested prior to the great day. The young father was instructed to ask the hospital nursery for a little unlaundered shirt the baby wore, which was then given to Chateau. He was enchanted with the little garment, slept with it for a few days and got used to it. He was encouraged to investigate the nursery, the new furniture, toys, and clothing of the baby.

When the little girl was brought home, the only people present were the parents and myself. No relatives, friends, neighbors, or visitors were allowed and the atmosphere was kept calm, quiet, and happy. The mother greeted the big dog properly when she got out of the car, then sat on the sofa with the baby on her lap. We held Chateau on a loose leash and allowed him to go near her, sniff her, and investigate the little newcomer. He was constantly told quietly that he was a "good boy" and a "gentle boy." Chateau was allowed to satisfy his curiosity after which he proceeded to "deflea" her gently but with dedication. When he finished, he licked her head and with a happy sigh, settled next to them on the carpet, placed his enormous head on his paws, and accepted both the situation and the strange looking new puppy. He was taken off leash, *supervised with the baby,* and then life went on as before.

The little girl found a champion in Chateaubriand. When the mother nursed her, he would position himself at her feet and no one could interrupt or disturb the nursing until the baby finished. He also changed his sleeping place from the parents' room to the rug in front of the crib, and if the baby stirred or whimpered, he went to get the parents and insisted that they come and look, right now! When the baby was taken out for a walk, there went Chateaubriand, strutting on his leash, the proud and devoted guardian. No

stranger could touch that pram! When he grunted a warning, no one in his right mind would force the issue.

The parents were delighted with their pet for accepting and caring for the baby. They understood that Chateau's attitude and behavior was very much due to their own attitude and sensible behavior toward the dog in this situation. They realized that Chateau's licking was neither dangerous nor carrying contagion, that the baby can always be washed, and that such activity is a vital part of recognition, identification, acceptance, and affection for the dog. If these are deliberately or unknowingly thwarted, the situation can turn into dangerous frustration and anger.

Caitlin (the baby in this case) is now four years old. She learned to walk by hugging Chateau's neck. She uses him as her pillow, knows how to "make nice," and handles him gently with no grabbing or pulling. If any should occur, the giant dog handles such roughness with patience, and judicious withdrawal from the scene.

When the young couple's second baby was born, Chateaubriand was a seasoned, experienced, and dedicated veteran of baby and child care. Creating a happy situation where a close and enduring bond develops is not difficult and need not be scary. It is a pleasant endeavor that is beneficial to the whole family.

So far we have dealt with introducing a new baby to an established animal. Another area where a happy and safe situation must be created is between dogs, crawlers, and toddlers. As was previously noted, it is rare that established dogs would harm an infant if the introduction is done correctly and sensibly, with a degree of caution used until the bond is formed. The situation changes when the baby begins to crawl, toddle, and move about. This is a new equation for the dog. This is no longer the helpless infant whose scent he knows, who just lies there and used to be sniffed and even licked! This little creature now *moves* about, looks different, and *smells* different (because her diet changed). Even her diapers may have a new, unfamiliar odor, and her voice may not be the same. Thus, the crawler is now someone new.

This baby is bigger and stronger and can grip, poke, hit, and cause pain. This baby's grip is strong and hard to release, hard to escape from when the little hand closes convulsively on an ear, a handful of fur, a muzzle, or a tail. At times, the child can only reach the genital area, and obviously this can leave a dog in serious pain!

A toddler presents an additional problem: she is unsteady on her feet. She will forge ahead relentlessly and in the process, falls a lot. The dog is wary, especially if the toddler has fallen on him several times before, usually when he was asleep. Or a toddler will throw herself on the resting dog in an effort to play or show affection. This startles a dog who may be coming out of his sleep and disorients him for a few seconds. He perceives the collision as an attack and lashes out.

Toddlers have a way of advancing on a dog in play and often cornering him. The dog often will not tolerate being cornered, and he is likely to come out of the corner either knocking the toddler over or delivering a warning nip or bite. Most dogs will warn prior to a nip or a bite, but the toddler does not understand this and keeps on going. When the nip occurs, the dog will take the blame.

Many parents think that a dog *must* tolerate anything a child metes out. In fact, many owners are proud of the fact that their dog allows the child to do anything to him, until the unfortunate day when the dog is really frightened and reacts unfavorably. At that point, disappointment, fear, and anger take over and the dog is eliminated by whatever means, even by destruction.

All this can be avoided. The education of the child is of paramount importance. If the child's training starts early enough—and there is no reason why it should not—nips and bites can be avoided, and a good relationship between the two can be encouraged and developed safely for both.

Too often the parents reaction to a warning growl is to rush on the scene and snatch the child out of reach, startling both toddler and dog. This is a wonderful way to teach a child to be afraid of dogs. It is also a wonderful way to teach the dog to dislike the child. This can also become a great attention-getting device by the child. The next time this happens, the child will not stop because all she has to do is get the dog to growl. Mother is sure to run to her and comfort her again.

Scolding the child in the dog's presence is also unwise. An intelligent dog will perceive that the child was at fault and the next time will take it upon himself to discipline him, which is what happens in a litter of puppies, because dogs learn by imitation. This is called *allelomimetic* behavior and is very much a part of the dog's personality. He may also get the idea that the scolding was directed at him, which then becomes an excellent reason to dislike the child. Dislike toward the child becomes even more acute when the dog is physically punished, tossed out, yelled at, or all of the above. If the dog now shows hostility toward his tormentor (the child) it is called *redirected* anger. He can't do much about the adult's behavior, but he sure can handle a small person.

Educating a child before she starts to move about is not only wise and safe, but it also establishes a solid foundation for learning kindness toward the family dog or cat, and a future humane attitude toward all animals. This is the best kind of education she can get. Kindness to animals is only a small step away from kindness, compassion, and consideration toward all living beings. This is also an excellent way to prevent a child from growing into a bully who becomes a most unpleasant and unattractive member of society. A child with the right kind of education will be instrumental in reassuring the family dog that children should not be the cause of fear, withdrawal, or hostility. My own dog came to me when he was two years old and was absolutely terrified of children. I can only imagine the abuse he must have endured from children.

The story of Vulcan covers two subjects: one, the problem of food guarding (this was discussed in Chapter 4); and two, the behaviors that are taught, or not taught, to young children. The method advocated by some, that of snatching food away, can become perilous. Here we will discuss how such exercises are unnecessary when a little education, restraint, and control over the child's actions can save a lot of wear and tear on all members of the family, including the dog.

CASE OF THE AIREDALE WHO GOT NO RESPECT

Vulcan was a large, handsome Airedale whose family included parents and two young children, aged six and four. His disposition was calm, sweet, and protective toward the children from whom he took and gave a normal amount of love and some loving abuse. Lately, however, Vulcan had occasionally growled at the younger child, and the parents sought help to stop this inexplicable behavior on his part. While consulting with the family, Vulcan was calm and tolerant. But when the younger child went over and picked up Vulcan's empty food dish to use as a toy, the dog tensed slightly. We immediately removed the dish and put it out of sight. After some questioning it became clear that Vulcan was fed sometimes here, sometimes there, but rarely in the same place. I requested that they feed the dog his dinner a little early while I was there so I could observe his behavior while eating.

As soon as Vulcan began to eat, the four year old went up to him, pushed him, leaned on him, nudged him, and generally harassed the dog. I asked that the child be removed immediately from the vicinity of the eating dog after I pointed out Vulcan's increasing nervousness. Upon more questioning it was found that Vulcan never exhibited any anger or distress at any other time. It was *only* when he was eating.

I asked the parents, "How would you feel if someone was constantly harassing you during your meal?" The answer was obvious. So then why allow the child to do exactly that to Vulcan? He too deserves respect for his needs and consideration while he is having his dinner.

The parents saw that by placing themselves in Vulcan's paws, they could easily relate to his problem. They did not permit the children to disturb anyone's meal, so Vulcan had to receive the same considerate treatment. It was also suggested that Vulcan get his meals in a quiet, out-of-the-way spot and always in the same place. The children were not to go near him until he had finished, and when he had, his empty dish was to be removed and put away.

The six-year-old understood the message Vulcan was trying to communicate. The younger child was simply not permitted near the dog while he was eating. Vulcan became his sweet, gentle self again in no time at all, never growling, never threatening, and of course he never nipped anyone. He now receives the same respect and consideration as the other members of the family.

When a decision is made to adopt an adult dog into the family, I applaud the family! When there are adorable puppies to choose from, it is easy to skip over the young adults who may have lost their "puppy-cutes." Giving a life to such a dog is rewarding—no housetraining, no teething to struggle through, more common sense and less youthful exuberance.

Had Pellucidar's family done their homework, they would have chosen an adult dog whose history and background were not completely shrouded in mystery. As rewarding as adopting an adult can be, it can also carry with it built-in problems that the new owner may not be aware of. Advice was not sought in orienting the dog to his new family and surroundings, so several problems resulted. The family banished the dog to the backyard every time visitors came, making the dog hostile and aggressive toward strangers. In addition to this situation, the children had no idea how to play with him and no one knew what to do when Pellucidar exhibited nervousness in the children's presence.

CASE OF THE BANISHED DALMATIAN

Pellucidar was a three-year-old neutered male Dalmatian who had lived in several homes through the efforts of a rescue organization. He became so insecure as a result of this revolving door experience that when he finally ended up with the family I visited, he was fearful and extremely nervous around children.

When consultation was requested, I met an overly cautious and somewhat ambivalent animal. Pellucidar's history consisted of adoption into at least four homes, each dumping him back to the rescue group. Since he was placed with less care and preinvestigation than would have been wise, the group had no idea why he was repeatedly brought back. Obviously no one bothered to find out what the problem was, let alone work with him. All they knew was that Pellucidar was uncomfortable around children. It is fortunate that such careless and unknowledgeable rescue groups are rare.

At the time of the consultation the family consisted of parents and two boys of nine and seven years. Observation cleared up several points: because the children did not know how to play with Pellucidar, he was teased a lot. For example, he adored chasing a ball, but he had none to play with. When the children played with *their* ball, the dog was not allowed to play with it. When other children were visiting, he was banished to the yard again so that he would not be underfoot.

The problems were handled one at a time. When asked why Pellucidar had no toys or a ball of his own, the older boy stated that he had only one ball, which he did not wish to give up. Since the home was in an affluent neighborhood, I suggested that they could purchase a ball for the dog, as well as some other suitable toys. I taught the children how to play with Pellucidar, and within half an hour, he was happily chasing a ball and bringing it back. And because he was exiled to the yard when the children's friends visited, we now included them in the games. In a short time the dog began to relax and look forward to the young guests. All went well when I checked back in two weeks, four weeks, and three months later.

When I called again in six months, I was informed that Pellucidar had been returned to the rescue group again. The parents had grown lax in their continuing observation of the conditions, and the children decided that it was more "fun" to start teasing him again. They raced around, screamed, refused to play with him in a sensible way, and generally made his life miserable.

CASE OF THE CROWDED DOBERMAN

Sombra, a smallish female Doberman, and her brother Hidalgo were ten weeks old when they began their basic obedience program with me. They appeared to be in an ideal home with lots of space and a large yard and gardens to exercise and play in, all properly fenced and made secure. The family also owned a small Terrier and had two children, aged three and eighteen months.

The puppies progressed through the program with excellent results. Hidalgo was a quick pupil, learned well, and was eager to show off his new skills. Sombra was a more sensitive and more contemplative little lady. She was bright and performed what was asked of her in a magnanimous manner. By the time the pups graduated, Hidalgo was a loving clown of a dog and Sombra became the model of intelligent obedience and generous disposition.

There were three problems in the home that the Dobermans had to deal with. Hidalgo handled them with success, but Sombra experienced difficulties. First, the Terrier, being the established pet, bullied and generally harassed the two pups. The owners were advised and taught how to deal with the situation to reassure the Terrier that he was not threatened by the puppies' presence. This was *not* done. Hidalgo mostly ignored him, but Sombra soon could not take the little terrorist's attacks on her legs and the barking. She was tense when the Terrier was in the same room with her.

The second problem was that the owners' did not provide the pups with a doggy-door, which would have given them the freedom to come and go, not only for the purposes of elimination, but also to get away from the smaller dog. Because they had no free access to the outdoors, there were times when they had no alternative but to eliminate in the house on expensive Persian carpets. When the door to the yard was left open, there were never any accidents. As for actually teaching them correct toilet habits, this was left to the housekeeper, who did not always have the time or the inclination to cope with the problem.

The third trouble was the most severe, and again, it was the parents' failure to educate the children, particularly the three-year-old. He repeatedly stepped on Sombra's feet, believing this to be a great game. He was never admonished for such behavior. Whereas Hidalgo was more blasé about all this and simply removed himself, Sombra, who was nervous enough from the Terrier's attacks, could not deal with this additional stress and abuse. Finally, one day she growled at the child to warn him off.

Naturally, the parents were petrified. Suddenly in their eyes, Sombra became vicious, dangerous, and above all, *ungrateful* for all the good things they had given her. They refused to see that the dog had had enough and was merely *warning* the child, and that this could have been corrected by correcting the boy's behavior.

While I do not believe that the answer to a human or environmentally created problem is getting rid of the dog rather than dealing with the causes, in this case I gladly agreed to help re-home Sombra, precisely because her owners were unable or unwilling to understand her needs and that the two Dobies handled the stress in *two different* ways because they were *two different* dogs.

For Sombra's sake, I introduced her to a young man from a nearby town. It was love at first sight! She seemed to sense that this young man was willing to give her a quieter and calmer lifestyle, a home where she would be the only companion with no added stress of a noisy Terrier and an unsupervised child. When the time came to leave, she willingly jumped into his car (much to the amazement of her now-past owners who were convinced of her "ingratitude") and rode away, reclining on the back seat with her head trustingly in my lap.

When I checked on the two about a month later, the new partners had developed a close and loving bond. The young man's work allows him to take her with him and she has become his loyal, protective, and loving companion. She played happily with him and was relaxed with people in general, although she still avoided small children.

After a six-month check-back, Sombra had become far more comfortable with children. She had become a sensitive and intuitive dog with a delightful sense of humor. Sombra was happy, and so was her new friend.

Too many times the problems of overcrowding and a chaotic atmosphere in a home create the same response in animals as they do in people. Both become tense, grouchy, and short-tempered when their limited privacy is constantly invaded. In a home where there is an established pet, this is an important consideration. If there are small children in that same home, then intelligent handling of the problem becomes imperative.

Poor Freya was long-suffering from her little boy's expression of love, but once discovered, it was hastily corrected and trouble avoided.

CASE OF THE SUFFERING MASTIFF

Thor was a huge, two-year-old neutered Bull Mastiff. He was a magnificent example of his breed with a gentle disposition. He was excellent with the owners' fifteen-month-old son and he was the living embodiment of a responsible caretaker. In fact, when the child got tired or restive, Thor would lie down with his front legs extended so that the boy could crawl between them and fall asleep under Thor's massive head and chin. While the boy napped, Thor would not move a muscle.

About a year before I met them, another Bull Mastiff was added to the family. The female, Freya, was spayed by that time. A little smaller than Thor, she was still of a formidable size. Thor never showed any signs of jealousy and was not threatened by her presence. However, when Freya was petted by the adults in the home, he would gently interpose himself between her and whoever was attentive to her. Because both animals were affectionate and treated with equal attention, this never became a serious problem.

Freya was also gentle with the child, although not quite as patient as Thor. The mother was pregnant again, and it was touching to see Freya go to her and lean her head against the mother's abdomen, as if listening and waiting for the new child to arrive.

The consultation took place because Freya frightened the parents considerably. She was in the living room with the boy when the mother (who was in the kitchen, just a few feet away) heard Freya growl thunderously, followed by the child's crying. She rushed in, found absolutely no injuries or marks on the boy and realized that he was crying with fright. She admonished Freya who quietly moved away.

Upon observation, nothing indicated the cause of Freya's behavior. She was the same as always, attentive to the boy, listening to the sounds of the unborn baby, snuggling with her owners and with me while Thor was busy looking after the toddler. Then suddenly the reason became very clear. The child stopped, threw himself on Thor's back with a happy roar of "good doggie" and attempted to grab the dog's penis, which Thor would not permit. I asked whether the child had ever done something like this with Freya. He had occasionally. When this last incident occurred, it happened to be a cold and rainy morning.

An hour of discussion followed during which the parents were advised that even small children must be educated in animal care. They must be taught what can and cannot be done to and with a dog, and that there are limits even with gentle giants like Mastiffs. While the genitals of a dog, particularly of this size, may be fascinating to a small child, they should never be handled by rough little hands that grip strongly and can hurt such a sensitive area. Hurling of little bodies on top of unwary dogs can startle them and the response can easily turn into a tragedy.

Because of the details, it was strongly suggested that Freya be examined by her veterinarian to determine if there was any problem which could cause discomfort in the hip area. This was done and arthritis was found. Treatment was immediately begun.

The owners realized the validity of the recommendations and embarked on a teaching program for the boy. He was taught how to touch and not to touch Thor's and Freya's bodies, how to stroke and pet them without causing fright or pain. It was also suggested that the mother supervise the child with the dogs to make sure that he would not repeat his earlier performance and did not subject either dog to unsuitable handling and play.

Having checked back in one month, Freya never displayed any more threats or warnings. The little boy was taught in no uncertain terms what was appropriate play. Thor and Freya were stable and well adjusted. At that time, Freya was still engaged in "baby listening."

Follow-up was done three months later. Everything was going well. The new baby arrived—a little girl—and Freya took charge and became her devoted keeper. To see the two giants resting on their elbows, each with a child in their care was a wonderful experience.

In conclusion, an important point must be made on the subject of children and animals. Day in and day out I am told by clients that the dog was acquired "to teach the children responsibility." This is one of the *worst reasons* to give a child an animal. Teaching responsibility is the parents' job, *not the dog's!* In fact, all parents should be aware that the ultimate responsibility of caring properly for a family pet is theirs, not the child's.

It is rare, indeed, that a six- or seven-year-old child is able to consistently care for a dog's every need. It is rare even with older children. It is also rare that the child's interest remains steadfast over long periods of time. Feeding, grooming, exercising, and emotionally supporting a dog is an effort that requires persistence, understanding, and a long-term commitment. To expect all this from a young child is unrealistic. I warn parents that unless they are willing to accept the responsibility for the animal's care themselves, they should reconsider. Don't create a situation where the child can easily develop an aversion and dislike for the animal who is being *used* to teach him something he may not be ready for or that the animal is unable to do. It is unfair to both the child and the dog.

The Do's and Don'ts of Dog Ownership

The following is an educational aid for use by families with children who are considering pet ownership or who already share their homes with animals. The list is not hard to remember and should be strictly adhered to.

DO:

- Respect your pet and his right to rest, peace, and privacy when he needs it.
- Give consideration to his need for clean and nourishing food, a constant supply of clean, fresh water, his own toys and bed.
- Protect him from the teasing, harassment, abuse, and cruelty by *your* human friends who do not understand the special friendship you have with your companion.
- Learn to work with adults in training and educating your dog, and use a light touch with him. Learn the basics of animal care and make sure that your friend is kept healthy, clean, and groomed, and has special playtime with you.
- Learn the danger signals when you meet strange dogs so that you can avoid misunderstanding, fright, and injury.
- Learn the body language of your dog so you can detect when he is not feeling well.

DO NOT:

- Try to stop a fight between dogs, whether they are your own or strangers in the neighborhood.
- Touch a strange or unknown dog, whether he is loose or with his owners, without permission.
- Disturb your dog when he is eating or sleeping.
- Carry food around—this is deliberate teasing.
- Put your face close to the dog's face suddenly. This will startle him. If the dog is one who doesn't know you, this can result in a fear bite.
- Scream and race around your dog. This will excite him and create hysteria, resulting in nipping and biting.
- Exercise a large dog without an adult to help in case he gets too hard to control.
- Kick or hit your dog, ever.
- Poke, grab, pull ears or tail, step on paws, ride or throw yourself on your dog, especially when he is eating, sleeping, or resting in hot weather.
- Stare at him long and intensely. This is a challenge and could result in an attack.
- Touch or play with any dog's genitals or genital area.

CHAPTER

The Home Wreckers

"**I** give him a good home, good food, exercise, veterinary care, love and toys, and he pays me back by destroying my home!" is a familiar, sad refrain I hear again and again.

"He knows he is doing wrong! The minute I walk in, he cowers and shows how guilty he is!" is the next.

"I'll get him a little buddy to keep him company. That will stop him!" is the next statement, supposedly a panacea.

All of the above refer to destructive dogs. I have seen damage done by tiny dogs that would make a Great Dane proud! I have seen what I call both generalized destruction (the entire house is attacked) or specific destruction (directed against a specific item or area). I have seen doors, walls, floors, screens, and furniture demolished that would put a tank to shame—well, a small tank, anyway.

What the owner fails to realize is that the dog is not repaying anything and certainly not this way. He is not spiteful. He does not take revenge. He has no idea that he did anything wrong and he is *not acting guilty*. Finally, a little buddy is not always the answer, because the problem could possibly double when the little buddy joins in the fun. Yet sometimes it does help, *after* the problem has been resolved.

Whenever destructive behavior occurs, I look at the objects, the location, the owners' routine, and above all, the dogs' physical and emotional environment. What is he unhappy about? What is he missing? What is he trying to say?

The keys to such behavior are *when, where, what,* and *why*. We know that a teething puppy chews. We anticipated it, sympathize with it, accommodate and ease the discomfort as much as we can. We also know that once the permanent, adult teeth are in, this kind of chewing will stop. But when it does not stop and the cute little teeth are not cute or little any more, then they become efficient tools that create havoc.

There are countless reasons and circumstances that cause dogs to destroy things. Loneliness, isolation, hunger, insecurity, boredom, and the relief of stress are all reasons. Chewing for a dog serves the same purpose as a pacifier serves a small child. It relieves stress and tension, hence the name pacifier. Destruction is never done for spite or vengeance. It is done to achieve a result. It can also be caused by what is now given a fancy name: separation anxiety. This simply means that Chester really doesn't want to stay at home alone while you go out for eight to ten hours. And why he doesn't want to stay alone depends a great deal on your behavior and interaction with Chester when you are at home with him.

The unmistakable symptom of this kind of destruction is that it *never* occurs when Chester is *with* someone. It is not because he is sneaky, spiteful, or stubborn, but simply *because he is not alone.* That is the result Chester was aiming for—*not to be alone!* It is the "aloneness" that elicits the behavior, not spite, vengeance, or ingratitude. By the way, spite, vengeance, and ingratitude are eminently human characteristics! They have no place in the psychology or logic of an animal.

Homewrecking can be easily encouraged by the owner himself—if they feel that being alone is unpleasant, scary, and difficult, and I suspect they attribute these feelings to Chester. Thus, before they leave the house they put on a formidable act of consoling him, preparing him for the unhappy experience before he is actually alone. Upon return, another performance takes place, that of apologies for having left, great joy at coming home, guilt for inflicting such unpleasantness on Chester, and generally greetings that would be appropriate if the owner had been away for months instead of hours. In short, the dog is deliberately set up to expect something unpleasant (by the owner's attitude) rather than accept the owner's presence and temporary absences as facts of life, a part of daily living.

Also, it sounds obvious, but tidiness is a great help. A dog will not chew up shoes if they are out of reach! Of course, giving Chester an old shoe is a mistake, because he can't be expected to know the difference between his old shoe and your $120 new ones.

CASE OF THE DESTRUCTIVE DOBERMAN

Lady was a beautiful seven-month-old spayed female Doberman who had been with her adoptive family for three weeks and adjusted well in every respect except one: during the night she demolished everything in the garden and in the garage where she slept. Plants, flowers, bushes, small trees, her bedding—nothing was safe.

The family had another dog, a white German Shepherd, who was a little older than Lady. She never exhibited such destructive tendencies. The Shepherd also slept in the garage. In fact, she preferred to be outside during the hot California nights. She was quite efficient in alerting the family of unusual noises or activities outside.

The family's thirteen-year-old son and Lady had became very close in the short time they had been together. Lady developed a strong but safe protective attitude toward the boy and *the interior of the house.* Lady did not show any other behavior problems and was not antisocial or hostile. Dobermans are particularly people- and owner-oriented. Because a close bond had been established between the dog and the son, I recommended Lady be allowed free access to the interior of the house at all times with the help of a doggy-door. I also suggested that she be allowed to sleep in the boy's room, with the door open to enable her to patrol the inside of the house and go out if she felt the need.

The suggestions were accepted and followed. A doggy-door was installed and Lady learned to use it in less than a half an hour. She now slept in the boy's room on her own blanket. The destruction in the garden and the garage stopped and never recurred. She protected the house inside while the Shepherd handled the outdoors. Lady's message was clear: "Let my friend the Shepherd guard the garden, and I will guard the home. I will also guard and protect you and your son."

On follow-up, the parents told me that Lady is as perfect a lady as can be expected. She also taught herself to take her own blanket, place it on the son's bed, and sleep there with him. Both boy and dog were happy with this arrangement and the parents could safely replant the garden.

Whenever I am called on a case where the owner is very busy with little time to spare for his companion, I am saddened at the plight of the animal. Dogs need interaction! Acquiring a dog and keeping him in the house or the apartment with no time allotted for him is unkind. The following case is a good example of this.

CASE OF THE ONE-DOG WRECKING CREW

Considering his size (all of four pounds!), Alonzo created havoc in his home that was of gargantuan proportions—holes in the carpet, decorator pillows gutted, chair legs gnawed (was this dog part beaver?), sofas disembowelled, drapes and curtains shredded. This animal was a one-dog wrecking crew. Alonzo was a two-year-old intact male Maltese in the peak of condition, very friendly and very social. He adored people and was a real charmer. He could sit up with lifted paws and head askance, and he could dance on his hind legs and do quite respectable pirouettes. He had a way of looking at you that really tugged at your heart. Alonzo was also lonely, bored, and emotionally abandoned.

Upon questioning it became clear that Alonzo's owner worked long hours and had a very busy social calendar as well. Consequently, Alonzo lived a solitary life and was suffering from emotional neglect. While some dogs respond to such lifestyle with lethargy and learned helplessness, others, like Alonzo, take a more active form of communication. It should have been clear to the owner that the little dog was sending desperate messages because this behavior never manifested itself when anyone was *with* him. It should have told her something, but obviously, it did not. Instead, she punished the little fellow when she came home and found the damage, cleaned it up in front of him and then left again "only to go out to dinner," or "just to the movies," or "had to go dancing."

I am certainly *not* condemning this owner's lifestyle. She had the right to live her life precisely as she wished and an animal behavior specialist's job is not to dictate lifestyles to anyone. But it *was* my job to explain that with such a heavy schedule of work, social activities, and frequent absences, her ownership of him was not an ideal situation for Alonzo. As he demonstrated, it was far from ideal for her, too. When she took the pup to work with her, he behaved like an angel and she lulled herself into a false sense of security that all would be well. When they came home and an hour later she would go out again, she invariably returned to disaster. She also never gave a thought to his possible unease in the darkness, to his loneliness, his boredom, and his feeling of emotional loss.

Because she did not wish to part with Alonzo, several recommendations were made after the causes for the dog's behavior were explained. Obviously, she could not take him everywhere. In this case, because he was enamored of the neighbor's cat, a companion was suggested. Perhaps another small dog or a kitten, introduced properly to avoid jealousy and resentment. It was also recommended that both Alonzo and the newcomer be altered (regardless of whether the new friend is a dog or a cat) Also, I recommended that the owner leave a light on when she's out at night, to prevent the animals' possible disorientation in the dark.

Feeding was to be done twice daily and a special time set aside for interaction with the pets without any distractions. Finally, a mild and aversive substance (inoffensive to humans), such as undiluted Listerine, was used to remind Alonzo that all marked objects, as well as those he was likely to try, were now off limits. However, no punishment was to be used and all damage was to be righted and tidied up in secret, with Alonzo and his friend away from the area.

Within a week Alonzo was neutered and a lovely little spayed female Maltese was correctly introduced to him as his new roomy and playmate. Two days after Mistinguette arrived, the two were fast friends, romping and chasing happily, only to collapse exhausted and sleep peacefully side by side. Alonzo lost all interest in attacking the home and everything in it, and the daily play and interaction with the owner did wonders to strengthen the bond between them. Mistinguette happily joined in the fun.

The twice daily feedings helped relieve the boredom and the tension created by an empty stomach and the anticipation of food. The pups utilized the nourishment better and peace and harmony prevailed in a short time. This was a happy situation where adding a friend helped rather than doubled the trouble.

The owner still had a busy career and social life, but she made it a priority to spend a little time with her dogs. She really began to enjoy the situation and this new relationship gave her a real understanding of the needs of companion animals. One year later, Alonzo had not attacked or destroyed anything in the apartment.

CASE OF THE CURIOUS TERRIER

About six months before I met her, Prudence, a six-year-old spayed female Wirehaired Terrier developed a habit that drove her owners to desperation. She would jump at the drapes, grab a mouthful of the fabric, and hang on until the material tore. She shredded two or three living room drapes in this way. She also damaged the carpet at the front door by scraping and scratching it with her front paws. Her companion, Percival, a year older than she and of the same breed, was according to the owners a perfect gentleman.

Because Prudence's problem was not a case of arrested juvenile chewing but something that developed long after that stage was over, her owners tried to break her of this habit. Their attempts were all physical and resulted in failure. During consultation several significant points were noted: 1) the owners had moved to their present home with the two dogs about six months before; 2) the home faced the oceanfront where the sound of waves and beachgoers was constant; 3) the drapes involved were always on the window facing the ocean; 4) there was a sofa under that window; and 5) the tear in the drape was always over the sofa's back.

The owners re-created for me the conditions under which the attack on the drapes happened. They left the house. Prudence jumped on the back of the sofa and proceeded to attack the drapes. As soon as Prudence could hear the owners coming back, she left the drapes, ran to the door and started to scratch and scrape the carpet until the owners came in. Once they did, both activities stopped abruptly.

Prudence was exhibiting a common canine characteristic when she was tearing the drapes: boredom. Percival's company was not quite enough for her especially when she heard the surf and the people outside who were far more interesting. However, the drapes were closed to protect the sofa from the sun and thus, she proceeded to make her own window. Once this was accomplished, she sat for hours on the back of the sofa, thoroughly enjoying the entertainment and the view the world outside was offering to her. As for the carpet scratching, this was excitement and release of tension pent up during the day after the owners left with lengthy good-byes. She was anticipating the hearty hello she was going to get. Percival was, indeed, the perfect gentleman! He let her do all the work and damage, while he calmly sat by and watched.

It was evident to the people that physical correction was not working. They tried it long enough without improvement and were eager to try another way. They understood now that the little Terrier was bored and created her own diversion. Therefore, it was suggested that the furniture be covered and the drapes left open for Prudence's convenience. They were more than willing to accommodate her in this respect. This had an added, unexpected bonus: once the drapes were left open, Prudence could see her owners coming home (not merely hear them) and instead of excitedly scratching the carpet, she would run to the door and wait until it opened.

Prudence no longer had to make her own window. Now she could perch on the back of the sofa and watch the goings-on outside. She has become a little celebrity in her neighborhood and people greet her as they go by. Prudence is now a perfect little lady and together with Percival enjoys the good life. So do their owners.

Destructive behavior is not confined to indoors. I've seen backyards that were booby trapped with holes of varying depths where it was easy to twist or break an ankle and impossible to keep a lawn or grow plants. Dogs dig for specific reasons. Northern breeds make shallow cooling holes. Bored dogs dig to amuse themselves. Some dig to hide a food treat. Others dig in response to the vibrations that gophers create under the surface. Some dogs will dig by the back door or under a bedroom window when locked out of the house. And some dogs dig because it is just so much fun!

Reasons for not allowing a dog in the house are legion: "He'll bring in fleas" (instead of addressing the flea problem, the dog is isolated). "He sheds fur" (instead of embarking on a simple brushing program). Grooming might be a cheap price to pay for not having the yard destroyed, not to mention losing the companionship and security he would provide inside. "He house-soils" (instead of housetraining him, he is locked out and *never* learns reliable toilet habits). "He is restless and wants to go in and out" (instead of using the "owner's best friend"—a doggy-door, which makes both areas accessible without the owner having to play the doorman). "Dogs are not supposed to be in the house"—says who? They were not meant to be domesticated either, but once we took them into our caves and homes and hearts, what is supposed to be is no longer clear-cut. Finally, "the children have allergies" (then why bring a dog home in the first place?).

CASE OF THE FORGOTTEN CHESAPEAKE

Chessie was a gentle eighteen-month-old spayed female Chesapeake Bay Retriever living with a young couple and their ten-month-old baby. About six months before the consultation the family moved into a house (from an apartment), and soon after Chessie started to urinate inside and dig holes outside, under the parents' bedroom window. Shortly after the move, the young wife indulged in her desire for as many pets as she could find, and so in addition to Chessie and the baby, now there were two cats, one parrot, one large turtle, two rabbits, several hamsters, and one Nubian Pygmy goat named Butter. When I saw the family, they were even thinking about adding more to the animal community in their home.

I asked them to go through their routine of caring for the animals in my presence. As soon as attention was given to one pet, Chessie would quietly place herself in front of the caregiver. She was then gently brushed out of the way until her turn came. On top of everything else, poor Chessie was now relegated to sleep outside because of the urination. Attempts were made by the couple to correct the urination with archaic methods: spanking, hitting with paper, pushing her nose into the mess—all to no avail. Of course, she became a little skittish. The only person Chessie was completely relaxed with was the baby.

We discussed that moving from an apartment to a house with a big yard was very good for Chessie, but it was a drastic change and a little unsettling. Before she had a chance to get used to the new surroundings, more and more animals kept arriving, and unavoidably, she got less attention than she did before. In fact, the only one who gave her undivided attention was the baby! Chessie felt forgotten!

Significant changes had to be made in Chessie's physical environment, starting with the installation of a doggy-door, which she learned to use without any trouble. She resumed sleeping in the baby's room. Any toilet activity outdoors was highly praised and, unless caught in the act, ignored indoors.

The most important change was made in the owners' interaction with Chessie. She became the first to be greeted, first to be fed, first to be petted. Every day, several short play periods were spent with her to the exclusion of the other animals. The improvement began to show in a few days. Indoor urination stopped completely and the digging dropped dramatically and disappeared within three weeks.

Life was pleasant for everyone. Chessie became calmer, happier, and more tolerant of the other pets, but I recommended that no more animals be acquired for a while.

Barriers can be made into terrifying objects. Matilda developed what I would call severe claustrophobia because of the trauma she suffered as a puppy. In her case, once her fear was overcome by her courage, intelligence, and her owners' compassion, the destruction stopped.

CASE OF THE CLAUSTROPHOBIC AUSSIE

An eleven-year-old female Australian Shepherd named Waltzing Matilda was destructive in a unique way. When left outside, she broke, chewed, and destroyed everything in her path in an effort to get inside the house. When left inside the house, she did the same in order to get out. When she finally chewed her way through a heavy aluminum grating protecting the door, breaking one tooth in the process and bleeding from a badly cut lip, her owners despaired and called for help. Considering Matilda's size, a mere 40 to 45 pounds (18 to 20 kg), the damage was astonishing and attested to extreme panic.

We discussed Matilda's past history from the day they acquired her at the age of eight weeks. She was brought home and the husband decided to make her an "outdoor dog." Matilda being very young and scared, away for the first time from her mother and siblings in new surroundings and without the warm, soft bodies she used to curl up with, whimpered, barked and "refused" to stay alone. The husband, intending to "teach her a lesson" put her in the doghouse and nailed some boards across the door to keep her inside. After three nights of this, her hysterical cries proved too much for everyone and she was allowed out. However, the damage was done and Matilda's barrier problem combined with claustrophobia was well established. It doesn't take much and it doesn't take long for a trauma to be created, and it is not easy (sometimes impossible) to overcome one.

Because Matilda had never destroyed anything other than barriers and doors in her path, a doggy-door was suggested to enable her to come and go as she pleased. This eliminated all the obstacles that terrified her and triggered the desperate need to eliminate them. The doggy-door was immediately installed. She learned to use it without fear or apprehension, and three days after its appearance, she was left alone in the house for a few hours. Absolutely no damage was done and Matilda waited patiently for her owners to return home.

Matilda chewed the doorsill only once after the door was in place, when a gun was discharged repeatedly nearby. Apart from that one incident, there has been no destruction. Matilda negotiated doors calmly and without fear.

Sometimes a dog will do what appears to be destruction when in fact, it is not. Janus scratched the carpet only when he was about to lie down. Had the owner in the following case known more about the breed, she would have realized that Pulis do this in the field where they work, before they lie down. This is called rooting (or nesting).

CASE OF THE RESTLESS PULI

Janus was a year-and-a-half-old intact male Puli whose owners doted on him. Janus could do no wrong, except one thing—he had a habit of madly scratching the carpet with his front paws. The carpet was getting threadbare in some spots. The owners sought advice from trainers, to no avail.

Having observed Janus for a while, his behavior had a definite purpose, and it soon became clear what he was doing—Janus was nesting! The owners did not know enough about this particular breed of dog, so some education in this area was undertaken. The Puli is a phenomenally talented dog. To watch a good Puli working a herd of sheep can easily humble the observer. He does his job with innate intelligence, planning, and strategy, and follows signals with understanding and consideration.

Although he spends most of his life outdoors with the herd and the sheep-herder, the Puli is also an equally ideal companion. But because he spends so much time in the field with no bedding provided for him, he scratches and softens the ground to make himself a comfortable place to rest or nest. Actually, many breeds do this but Pulis are particularly talented in this area.

The routine Janus followed was circle-scratch-lie down-get up-circle-scratch-lie down- get up, and so on, for about 10 to 15 minutes until he was satisfied with the spot he prepared and then he would settle for a good nap.

Janus was allowed to sleep anywhere in the house except on the furniture. No bedding in the form of a basket or blanket was provided for him, but he slept on his owners' bed at night if he felt like it. After the behavior was explained, it was recommended that a bed of sorts be given to him in the form of a large basket, pad, or at least his own blanket. Then left to his own devices, he would handle the situation. This was done and within a week Janus was happily scratching, pushing, nudging, and rearranging his blanket after he dragged it to various areas in the house. Once he felt that it was arranged just right, he would go to sleep.

Janus never indulged in carpet scratching again and finally when the house was recarpeted, Janus completely ignored the floor and continued to nest on his own comfortable blanket.

Drastic changes in a dog's life are as upsetting as they are in ours. Emotional divorces are more so because in addition to the highly charged atmosphere and physical change of location, one of the "parents" also disappears. Because of the deep attachment a dog forms to his owners, this can be terribly upsetting and scary.

CASE OF THE UPSET AKITA

Mingo, a four-year-old male Akita, lived with his "parents," a husband and wife. He was a happy-go-lucky, well-adjusted dog. The wife called for a consultation after Mingo repeatedly chewed the furniture "suddenly and out of the clear blue sky." The visit was arranged for the weekend so that I could meet the working owners.

Mingo was friendly, powerful, and exuberant, overflowing with affection and high spirits. The damage to the furniture was considerable and Mingo was beginning to diversify! Although the target of his attentions was primarily the sofa, he was now having a go at the chairs and tables. Upon extensive questioning, it was determined that none of Mingo's actions happened suddenly or out of a clear blue sky.

Two months before I met him, Mingo's life had changed dramatically. His owners divorced, the wife moved into a new home, started to work, and to keep Mingo from getting lonely, a new pet was added, a young female Labrador Retriever named Fritta. Such drastic changes occurring over a short period of time could easily unsettle a dog. Mingo had a lot to contend with and get used to.

Because Mingo had no obedience education at all, it was difficult for the wife to establish her leadership with him. If Mingo had a leader at all, it was the husband who was not present in his life now. Mingo naturally stepped into that vacated position. He was very fond of the husband and missed him. He was now suddenly left practically alone during the day without his lady's company. To add stress on top of stress, he was given a puppy who unsettled him a little more. He was not hostile to Fritta, the Labrador pup, he just ignored her eager attempts to play.

Education in basic obedience was suggested for Mingo so that leadership could be taken from him and assumed by the wife. Fritta was educated at the same time. Daily exercises in obedience served this purpose because now the learn-to-earn could be activated. It was established in his mind that no matter how downcast in the morning and how exuberant in the evening he may be, departures and arrivals were now unemotional. A mild aversive substance was used on the furniture merely to remind Mingo that chewing was not desirable as before.

The program proceeded well and in six weeks Mingo was far more relaxed and calm. The big change was in his behavior during his lady's absence—the chewing stopped. Play with Fritta started and life became pleasant for everyone in the home. For the last year Mingo has had nothing unauthorized in his mouth—except occasionally Fritta's ear or leg in the heat of play, which the wonderful Labrador tolerates with good-natured stoicism.

Destructive behavior can be truly traumatic to the owner. I can't think of anything more upsetting than having a brand new or favorite piece of furniture demolished by a beloved dog. I know! It happened to me! Upon discovery, my Taffy was not quite so beloved for a few moments. I took a few deep breaths, sat down and gave some thought to the reason she found it in her heart to commit such a criminal act. Sure enough, there it was! We just moved into our first house, the movers laid all the boxes and furniture helter skelter and after they left, we decided to go out for dinner because the kitchen was not yet operational. Poor Taffy, having just been taken from the apartment, the only home she ever knew and felt safe in, found herself in a strange place, unfamiliar, unexplored, alone in a physically and emotionally chaotic environment. She wasn't even sure where her blanket was placed! Shame on *me*! Taffy was reacting out of stress and fear.

An important word about using drugs to treat destructive behavior: For years, drugs have been used on our animals for a variety of reasons: for fear of thunder, fireworks, or explosions; to calm "hyper" dogs (who are merely energetic, overactive, and in most cases quite young); to calm dogs who bark too much. There is a veritable supermarket of drugs available for such uses. Before considering any psychotropic drug, be aware that unless you work with your dog on the behavior itself and understand that it takes time and involvement to change an unwanted situation, the drugs will not work by themselves. They may sedate, suppress, make sleepy or disorient the pet, but they will not eliminate the behavior. In fact, responsible manufacturers of such drugs *recommend* that behavior work is done and the drug used as an adjunct to such work. There are *no* magic pills!

CHAPTER

8

The Realm of Their Fear

Chapter 4 is titled "The Realm of Our Fear" and deals with our fear of canine aggression. Now I would like to talk a little about what dogs are afraid of, what causes *their* fears, the way they show it, and how they can be helped by willing and perceptive people in their lives.

Wild animals fear predators, threats to their young, fire, earthquake, flood, thunder, lightning, noise of any kind, and man. Deer often go into deep shock when chased by noisy snowmobiles or low flying helicopters. Their fear is compounded by the unnatural chase and many have literally died of shock and heart failure.

Our companion animals living with us in our homes are no longer fearful of predators and hunters. In their present environment their fears have changed to resemble many of our own. Dogs are afraid of specific sounds or people, other dogs or cats, traumas, inhumane and brutal treatment, confinement, wide open spaces—the list is long and complicated.

My feeling for a fearful dog is pity and the desire to alleviate the sad situation and the unfortunate results it can bring about. It is up to us to prevent fearful experiences for our companions in the same way that we prevent them for our children. Since through domestication and specialized breeding we keep them in a state of perpetual infantilism and total dependence on us for their physical and emotional well-being and health (the behavior of a domesticated adult dog is the same as that of a juvenile wolf), we owe them freedom from fear to the best of our abilities. A fearful child can be treated and reasoned with, but a fearful dog can become dangerous (fear biter) and that can cost him his life.

My objective in any case I consult on is a solution of the problem. I am also realistic enough to know that a problem is not always solvable, and in that case, I look for a way to *manage* the problem. Let me describe dealing with the most prevalent fears dogs experience, that of thunder and similar noises. One was solved successfully, the other was managed.

CASE OF THE HYSTERICAL SHEPHERD

Lyra was a ten-year-old female German Shepherd with mild dysplasia in one hip. She was gentle and good natured for all the power her size conveyed.

She was companion to two elderly cats (in addition to her human family) whom she mothered devotedly all her life.

Her owners called because Lyra had a serious problem with fireworks, thunder, backfiring cars, and any sudden loud noises. Her fear brought on mild psychomotor seizures. She raced around hysterically, crashing into funiture, doorways, and walls until she collapsed exhausted, and hyperventilating. The only control the owners managed to devise was to push her to the ground and lie on top of her until she relaxed.

The family's history told the tale: When Lyra was six months old, they were invited to a Fourth of July fireworks display. They took the puppy with them and when the explosions began, Lyra became uneasy, yelped once or twice, salivated a little, and shook a bit. The couple then put on an Oscar-winning performance of babying, fondling, stroking, pitying, and "loving her out of it." Then they had a spectacular argument about exposing Lyra to such a traumatic experience. The results were predictable. From that time, any sound that reminded Lyra of fireworks, explosions, or rumblings, would find her owners poised and waiting for her reaction. Lyra was ready to oblige any time! They were busy stressing each other and finally when Lyra became hysterical, they called for help, fearing that she would injure herself. There was one question uppermost in my mind: Why did they allow this to go on for *nine and a half years?*

The owners were made aware of what had happened to Lyra and themselves at Lyra's first exposure to the noise. Although it is quite normal for a dog to show fright at such unexpected occurrences, their own behavior conveyed to her that it was perfectly all right to be frightened and that she was going to be rewarded for the fear with attention and affection.

At my request, the husband hid in the kitchen, blew up a paper bag, and then exploded it. Lyra became frightened and ran around the house a bit, but since the sound was not repeated, she settled down uneasily. They had purchased a recording of thunder some time before (but were not very successful with it), so I asked that it be played at a very low volume. Lyra became slightly nervous again. I increased the volume slightly and we left the room to sit in the kitchen, talking and laughing, being jolly and happy so that Lyra could hear us. With the thunder still going on, Lyra stopped the nervous wandering about and came to the kitchen to investigate what it was she might be missing. She ignored the sound as she approached and on arrival in the kitchen she was given the command *good sit!*, which was praised, then a *good down!* which was again praised, and finally a *stay!*

After a few minutes we stopped the recording and analyzed what happened. Lyra's episodes of fear were, to a great extent, reaction to her owners' behavior. Most certainly, after the first episode they actually taught her to behave as she did. Had they handled it calmly, nonchalantly, and with a minimum of attention to the fear, Lyra's life would have been free of this stress, not to mention their own.

Further exercises were recommended and my instructions were followed. This was in October. During the following months of rain, lightning, and thunder Lyra's fears slowly but surely lessened. Considering her age and the duration of her problem, chances are that she will never recover completely. However, her reactions are far better controlled and life has become much easier for all of them.

Dogs can be fearful, nervous, and shy. One typical symptom is involuntary or nervous urination. This is not a matter of breaking housetraining. Given any stressful situation, uncontrollable urination may occur.

There are some "experts" who recommend punishing a dog for such incidents. This has never made sense to me. I correlate such cruel methods with punishing a bedwetting child. The more he is punished, the more the bedwetting persists.

What causes nervous urination? In puppies who have not been properly socialized, it can be brought on by a well-meaning person who will bend and hover over the pup and in a loud and hearty manner will shout "nice puppy!" The words make no difference—the manner of the encounter does! Imagine if you will, a tiny creature, unsure of himself and of his world, who sees a giant. Suddenly, this giant bends down, hovers over the little creature and at the same time a loud, booming voice resounds in his ears, startling him. Result: fright, loss of sphincter control and involuntary urination, after which the puppy takes off and hides in terror because he has learned that another giant will punish him—for what? He has no idea!

If you remember your childhood you may recall a relative who was a cheek-pincher. Cheek-pinchers grab a handful of the child's face, pinch it in a manner they perceive as affectionate, and bending down, boom at the child. The child is frightened and he hates it! As soon as he can, he escapes. The next time the cheek-pincher arrives, he will do his best to hide before he is pinched again. A puppy can't do that because he doesn't know when the giant will come and scare him again. So each time it happens, he loses control and involuntarily urinates again. What a dirty puppy! Right? Wrong!

It would be so simple to avoid such problems! But if the condition exists, with a little effort and commitment, it is not too late nor too difficult to correct. However, before any corrective program is started, it must be ascertained that the puppy has no physical or medical problems that would contribute to the problem.

An animal (like a child) will be more comfortable and feel safer with something or someone close to his own size. Therefore, if the giant would only squat down and quietly say "hello, Chester" or not talk to him at all but let the pup approach and investigate, such fright could be avoided. If the quiet squat approach is not helping at first, then simply don't approach at all. Let Chester approach you when he feels safe and secure enough.

As for punishing such involuntary urination, it is guaranteed to make the problem worse! Making a big fuss about it and yelling at the puppy in a misguided effort to stop him will only exacerbate the problem. Instead, ignore the incident, clean the area when the pup is not present, and concentrate on helping him build up his self-assurance, sense of security, and feeling of safety.

Another cause for nervous urination is brutal treatment. It is not unusual for instance, for a dog to come home from training school or from attack training camp and at the first stressful incident or fearful situation to squat and urinate (and sometimes defecate) in terror. Just the opposite of what he was supposedly trained to do, right? Certainly not the result the owner hoped and paid for! But not *every* dog is cut out to be a guard or "attack dog." Not every dog can handle the kind of training it takes, and not *every* training school or attack-dog camp uses proper, humane, and intelligent methods to train the dogs handed over to their tender mercies. This is yet another excellent reason *NOT to send dogs away to be trained by others*. It is far better if the owner-leader does the actual training rather than the hired trainer. But, if the trainer does most of the hands-on training, it should certainly *never be out of the owner's sight*.

In the following case, the causes of nervous urination are further described.

CASE OF THE SUBMISSIVE POMERANIAN

Bismarck was a ten-month-old neutered male Pomeranian whose owners were at a loss to understand his constant submissive (nervous) urination. He was completely housetrained, affectionate, and in every way was a good puppy but for this. When he was neutered in order to eliminate this problem (I wonder who recommended *this* as a solution?), and it did not work, they were apprehensive that Bismarck might be "retarded." I assured them that if the puppy could be housetrained, he was most certainly not retarded and a consultation was arranged.

Bismarck proved to be a well-cared-for, sociable pup. He was however, a pet shop purchase and consequently nothing was known about his background, litter behavior, or if any effort had been made to socialize him appropriately. He was the sad result of puppy mill breeding, and trying to trace his history proved futile. He was four months old when he was bought, and until I arrived, advice was varied and interesting. His veterinarian suggested that they leave it alone because he will outgrow it. Another "expert" recommended punishing him. Of course he did not grow out of it and punishment made things much worse. Now Bismarck lost control when anyone greeted him, bent down to pet him, or tried to pick him up, when he heard loud voices, or when his people came home. After a thorough medical examination where no physical cause was found, their new veterinarian (not the "he will outgrow it" one), referred them to me.

Bismarck met me at the door, and as soon as I saw him, I crouched down, stayed very still and *did not look at him*. He approached, sniffed curiously, and then carefully nuzzled my hand. At this point the owner, a rather tall and powerfully built gentleman, bent over and in a booming voice called the pup to him. Bismarck immediately lost control and dribbled on the floor, his tail wagging all the time. Now the man boomed "bad puppy!" and Bismarck urinated a little more, and his tail stopped wagging. The wife came rushing out of the kitchen and proceeded to clean the spot immediately while Bismarck was watching.

A discussion followed with the owners. I explained that what Bismarck was doing was *not* housesoiling. Bismarck's submissive display was similar to what puppies do following stimulation by their mother to facilitate elimination. When the mother licks the pups' stomachs and genital areas, the puppies lift a paw and respond with urination and defecation. Without such licking and stimulation, they cannot perform these two functions and they will die.

As puppies grow and are able to see, the licking is no longer necessary. However, the mother will look at them in a way that indicates that she intends to roll them over. This look elicits the same response as the licking did. This is also the way they are taught to be den-clean as soon as they are able to follow their mother to eliminate away from the nest or den.

As they grow older they gain control and no longer respond to their mother in this submissive way. If they are properly socialized, they will not display this kind of submissive urination again. An unsocialized puppy experiencing stress (and what pet shop puppy does not?) will lose control and not get over it unless correctly handled. In poor little Bismarck's case, this submissive behavior was arrested precisely for this reason.

I demonstrated that if I crouched, turned sideways, looked away, and at most whispered to Bismarck, he would approach at his own pace and not urinate. Then I asked the owners to do the same. With the wife, no urination occurred. I suggested that the husband not even whisper. It worked! At this point I also instructed them *not to bend or lean over* the little dog. The husband was asked not to boom at him either in anger or praise. Absolutely no petting was to be done, no reaching out with hands, no touching of Bismarck's head, no direct eye contact, and no treats. If he appeared to be calm, then a brief and light touch could be given with one finger, but only under the chin. If this resulted in urination again, then they were to stop and try again later. They were not to talk to the puppy during the next two or three days and then try a quiet "good dog."

Now came the next step: Once the pup accepted the gentle pet under the chin without urinating, in response to the "good dog" he was to be given a simple command such as *sit* and on compliance, rewarded with another quiet "good dog." This was to be done a few times daily.

Recommendations were also made in how to greet the pup at homecomings: *ignore* Bismarck for a few minutes as if he didn't exist, then crouch, wait until he approaches, pet under the chin, and say "good boy." This must become a routine and friends and guests were asked to do the same so that the puppy became used to anyone visiting the home.

Another crucial element in Bismarck's education was that *he must never see anyone cleaning up after him.* If he lost control at any time, it was to be ignored, the pup placed out of sight, and the accident cleaned up in secret. Once done, the pup was allowed back *as if nothing had happened.*

We also arranged for Bismarck to sleep in his own little bed in the owners' bedroom instead of the garage, and this also helped build up his sense of security. By the time our consultation was nearing its end, Bismarck felt so good about himself that he allowed me to pick him up—dry!

After three weeks the owners reported that "a new day had dawned"! Bismarck improved dramatically. With the assistance of friends, relatives, and neighbors, the episodes of nervous urination were almost a thing of the past. He was improving, he was sure of himself and even began to jump on his owners. It was recommended that because he was a small dog, that this be permitted for a couple of weeks and then corrected by *sidestepping* him and giving him the *good sit* command. This is an excellent way of teaching Bismarck that jumping is not rewarding. It also teaches the owner that kneeing a dog in the chest is not only counterproductive but also dangerous. In the case of this small Pomeranian, it would also require excellent acrobatic skills on the part of a rather large man. Within two weeks the jumping also stopped and the urination did not recur.

The owners were overjoyed. They understood the emotional structure of this problem and their frustration and anger dissipated. They were relieved that Bismarck was not retarded and that their concentrated effort with him created a better understanding and a deeper bond. They were also happy with their new veterinarian who knew that the pup's physical and emotional well-being needed equal care and treatment to correct this behavior.

There are, of course, other fears, more exotic, more unusual, and harder to treat. Often I meet dogs who were adopted at three to four months of age who are already terrified of men, or terrified of a hand, or of being touched on the top of the head or the neck area. *There is always a reason* for the fear. Viva's fear was unusual and it was not easy to help him over it. Time, compassion, and the willingness to understand were tools that worked best.

CASE OF THE MAN-HATING PUP

Viva was a five-month-old Doberman-X who came to his present family through a rescue group. He was found abandoned with his brother and two

sisters in a rusty oil drum in an alley, all starving and terrified. His brother died of gangrene in his paw and his sisters were adopted. So was Viva but he was brought back to the rescue group in two weeks because "he could not be housebroken." At the age of four months Viva came to live with his present owners. He was fearful when he arrived and it took time to reassure him. With intelligent and correct methods he was housetrained in no time at all and developed a close rapport with the *wife*.

Not so with the *husband*. Viva was terrified of him, kept his distance, and the minute the man moved, Viva would bark at him from a safe distance. It was not a vicious or even angry bark, more of a "please stay away from me" kind of bark. They were most unhappy about the situation and asked for help.

Viva was a well-fed, well-groomed, shiny, and sleek puppy. He was alert, curious, and affectionate with women. He came to me willingly and softly licked my hand. His physical environment was excellent: a large house with a large yard, secure fencing, and a doggy-door, which he used happily. When the husband came in, Viva started to whooffle-bark at him and backed away. When the wife sat in the living room where the husband was, the pup came to her through another room in order to avoid going near or past him, and settled next to her on the side away from the husband. There was a very good probability that in the first home where the pup was placed by the rescue group, he was frightened, hit, or abused by a man. The probability was excellent that all three had occurred. As we talked, it became apparent that

Viva needed time and patience to develop trust and learn that not all men present danger to him.

I suggested that the husband take an active part in Viva's care. To start with, he should give the dog one of his two daily meals. Do this so that Viva can see him placing the food for him, and even if he runs away at first, persist in giving him his evening meal.

Viva also had "nightmares." He would whimper, yelp, and thrash about in his sleep and the wife would rush to wake him. Instead, it was recommended that the husband gently place his hand in Viva's abdomen, apply very light pressure, and call his name softly. If the puppy continued to sleep calmly, leave him be. If he woke up and realized that the gentle hand belonged to the husband, he would associate him with the reassuring touch and realize that he was not someone to be afraid of.

The couple followed the instructions and gave Viva the time and patience he needed. It took about a month for Viva to allow the husband into the room without barking. In another two weeks Viva walked by him without fear and two months after my visit, he allowed himself to be petted on the side of his head. Viva also started his basic obedience program and was learning fast. The lessons were done by both husband and wife, and when he graduated, he responded affectionately and equally to both. He gained self-confidence and reassurance, and when they took their first vacation with Viva, he was the best-adjusted, affectionate, and eager dog that both husband and wife could have hoped for.

Vagabond had a good reason for his fear of traveling. He had my sympathy when I remembered the accident I had when my brakes failed. My face required stitches and my broken ribs hurt every time I took a breath. I spent four weeks in bed and when it was time to get back into the car and drive, I was terrified. I almost believed that I would never be able to drive again, and when I finally did, I was dreading having to use the brakes, expecting them to fail again. It's no wonder that Vagabond was afraid after his frightening experience in a car.

CASE OF THE FRIGHTENED TRAVELER

Contrary to his name, Vagabond was a terrified traveler. Whenever he got into his owner's car, he started trembling, his teeth chattered with fright, and he was salivating profusely. I was called for a consultation when the only option was to leave him at home, but that would deprive the owner of the dog's company, which he always enjoyed.

Vagabond was a nine-year old male TerriPoo, large and friendly. There was nothing wrong with him in the house or walking on his leash. Upon questioning, it seemed that all his life Vagabond traveled with his owner until about six months before I saw him. His fear began then about two weeks after an automobile accident. The owner stopped the van at a red light. Vagabond was sitting in his usual place on the sofa-type seat behind the driver's seat, when a drunk driver smashed into the van from the rear. The dog was thrown forward, went over the owner's head and hit the windshield (canine seat belts had not yet come on the market). Fortunately, neither the owner nor Vagabond had broken bones, but the dog suffered enough soft tissue damage and bruises to make him sore and ache all over.

The young man tried to calm Vagabond's fears by offering him treats the moment he entered the van and was extremely sympathetic whenever the dog started to tremble. He then gave more treats, the outcome of which was that the dog now tended to throw up. For the duration of the drive he constantly talked to Vagabond, but he was becoming tense himself, which of course, the dog sensed and reciprocated. When the chattering of the teeth started, he knew he was not helping his pet.

After getting extensive background information, I suggested that I take Vagabond for a short drive in *my* car. He jumped willingly on the front seat and showed great interest as I drove him around the block. I did not talk to him or try to divert his attention and no signs of fear or nervousness were apparent. Next, I asked the owner to join us, this time placing Vagabond in the back seat. I instructed the young man to talk to me only and ignore the dog. We went around again, in a different direction, and again, Vagabond was perfectly calm.

Now we decided to try the van, and we got in but did not start the engine. Vagabond was on the same seat he occupied on his travels. The owner told me that usually by this time Vagabond had been given several treats and he would start talking to him. I advised him to ignore the dog, just talk to me. After about five minutes I asked him to start the engine but not start driving. Vagabond grew a little tense, but soon relaxed. Vagabond was now given the command *down,* and when he complied he was briefly but enthusiastically praised. Then I suggested that we start driving.

At first we drove a few miles on the freeway to avoid traffic lights. Each time Vagabond showed any restlessness or tension, he was given the command *down* and praised for compliance. Then we got off the freeway and drove along city streets where we had to slow down, turn, and stop for lights. Vagabond was less nervous and within half an hour we could stop and go without any reaction from him. By the time we got back to the house, Vagabond was fast asleep in his seat.

We discussed what transpired here. The owner understood that when Vagabond began to show fear in the van, he—with the best intentions—unwittingly reinforced the fear by rewarding it with treats and excess sympathy. Thus, he *taught* Vagabond that the van was indeed a place to fear and the fear would be rewarded. What we did instead was convey to him that there was nothing to fear and if he showed any, it would not be rewarded. Instead of sympathy, he would be distracted by having to do something (*down*) and the reward would be praise. In a short time, Vagabond was so concerned with getting the praise that he forgot his fear. Such drives were practiced every day for longer and longer distances until the owner felt comfortable with giving the commands to Vagabond and until all fearful behavior disappeared. No miracles were expected, but time and consistency cured the problem.

Three weeks later I received a call from the young man. Vagabond was happily accompanying him again in the van, without trembling, without fear, and without chattering teeth or salivation. He got in and out of the van cheerfully and looked forward to the trips.

Many dogs are terrified in cars. I am not talking about puppy car-sickness, but actual terror when the motor turns over and the car starts to move. This is not always the result of a trauma, yet the fear is real and creates problems when the driver is also endangered by the hysterical animal. It happened to me when I first added Mr. Smidgeon to my family of companions. I found him in the middle of the road, a five-month-old ball of fur, a small dog whom I describe as a TerriWhip. The first time I had him in the car to go to the veterinarian, he jumped on the floor of the car, screaming, and took refuge under my left foot—the one that operates the brakes. I had two options: go through a red light or squash the little dog under my foot. Somehow I managed to avoid both, but the lesson was indelibly learned: work with the puppy and *get him a seat belt*.

The method was similar to the one used with Vagabond. We sat in the car a lot until he felt safe and relaxed. Then we got out and repeated this several times. When he was calmly sitting on the seat next to me, I started the engine and just let it idle. When he stood up he was given the commands *good sit* or *good down* and highly praised. Once he felt comfortable in the stationary car with the engine idling, I started taking him on short trips, which gradually grew longer until finally the fear disappeared. Now my Mr. Smidgeon travels like a seasoned veteran and loves every minute of it.

A dog should *never* ride with her head hanging out of the car window. There is always the danger that she may dive out of the moving vehicle, given sufficient motivation (another dog, a cat, a jogger). Flying dust and pebbles can injure the delicate tissues of the eyes, which results in suffering for the dog and a veterinary bill for the owner. A slightly opened window for air circulation is enough and doesn't endanger the dog. And of course, *never* leave the dog alone in the car for any reason. Even on a sunny winter day, the car becomes hot inside (hothouse effect), and the animal will suffer heat stroke with irreversible brain damage in a very short time that ends with death.

Another form of fear and dread for dogs is kennel syndrome, which can be similar to agoraphobia in humans. It usually happens when a dog has been kept in a kennel during the formative period of his life for so long that his prison becomes a safe haven. He is unable to deal with a lack of barriers and becomes terrified of open space. One of my dogs had a classic case of kennel-syndrome and her rehabilitation took the better part of a year. I was fortunate because I had three established companions at the time who became my co-therapists, and together we were able to eliminate this particular fear from her loving soul.

Nefer was rescued from a dreadful boarding kennel where she was abandoned as a puppy and kept in a cage for 11 months where she was forced to eliminate and lie in her own waste. As for food, she was certainly not spoiled and when I got her out of that awful kennel (which I helped to shut down and put out of business), she was mere skin and bones. She had to be rehydrated, and it took at least four baths to remove the dried feces from her coat and skin, and to eliminate the dreadful odor.

When I took her home, she almost went into shock in the car from fright. At home, I had to lift out a trembling, shaking dog who could barely stand up. She was uninterested in my other companions, Circe, Pip, and Sombra. Instead, she found a corner in the living room, collapsed and stayed there for the next three months. I made her a bed in that corner, and if I had not bodily carried her outside, she would have eliminated in that corner, too. No one could approach her for the first two weeks without causing a renewed fit of tremors, and she would not eat if anyone as much as looked in her direction. Circe, Pip, and Sombra took up their post around her and stayed with her day and night to reassure, comfort, and keep her safe. Her first interaction, in fact, was with them and their friendship endured until her death at the age of eight.

Housetraining was a challenge to her and to me. The doggy-door became a monster she could not cope with, but eventually, if the door was left open she would manage to step outside and eliminate—perilously close to the door. The most overwhelming fear she had (more than fear of freedom and fear of the doggy-door) was men! It was this apprehension that finally got her over her fear of the little door.

I asked my gentle son-in-law to help me teach her how to use the opening and while I called to her from outside, he very slowly and gently approached her on the inside, carefully herding her toward the opening. Finally, her fear of him overcame her fear of the door and she came through. Victory! From that moment on, she never failed to use the doggy-door and never had an accident inside the house again. She lost her fear of my son-in-law as well and till the day she died, he was the only man she was not afraid of, did not bark at, and asked for affectionate rubs, which he never failed to give her. She blossomed and developed a normal protective instinct, defending both me and the house with intelligence, valor, and courage.

Many times I've been asked whether it was worth going through the trouble and time her rehabilitation involved. To me it was well worth it! When I look at the pictures I took when I brought her home and compare them to how she was one year later, all I can think is that I'm glad I got her. Every night before she fell asleep on the love seat in my bedroom, I gave her a hug and whispered, "I'm glad I got you." If I forgot the nightly ritual, she would stand by my bed and wait…yes, I have gotten up to see her settled and then whispered to her the words she needed for reassurance. But you see, she gave me so much in return!

Tiny was easier to help over his fear. He spent considerably less time in isolation than Nefer, although his problem was compounded by lack of socialization. This is an essential part of bringing up an emotionally stable and healthy dog. Unless he is used to and is comfortable with other animals and humans, such a lack will translate into serious problems in the adult dog.

CASE OF THE IMPRISONED ROTTWEILER

Tiny was a large, intact male Rottweiler, a beautiful, massive dog who was brought home from a presumably knowledgeable breeder at the age of ten months. In his new home Tiny was not only shy but did his best to find secluded corners, burrow into them, and stay there at all times. He would reluctantly go to the yard to eliminate but only if dragged on a leash. Once he finished eliminating and was let off the leash, he would go back to his corner. Any efforts to get him to come out of his safe place and attempts to get him to follow his owners to another room proved futile.

When I met him, it was apparent that Tiny had never been socialized with people. When the breeder was contacted and asked whether the puppy was isolated from people at any time, he said that Tiny was kept in a cage to "keep him from getting under foot." His only contact with humans was when he was given food and water. No other interaction was done! When I asked him why did he not inform the buyers that this was an unsocialized pup who needed special attention and care, he retorted "what difference does it make?" As we've seen in case after case, it makes a big difference!

It was evident that the pup was suffering from kennel syndrome. Fortunately, Tiny happened to be innately good natured. He did not suffer any physical abuse, but the *emotional* abuse and neglect needed to be treated and several steps were taken to replace Tiny's familiar and secure prison with other forms of reassurance.

First, we had to get him out of the safe area he had selected. His food was offered in the middle of the kitchen so that he had to leave the corner. When he finally came and finished eating, he was happily but quietly praised. He was gently made to stay in whichever room the owners occupied, and toys were provided for him, especially chew toys.

Tiny was given his own bed in the owners' bedroom so that sleeping in close proximity gave him added security, reassurance, and the opportunity to get used to staying away from secluded corners. In addition, no excessive indulgence or too much attention was to be shown so that Tiny was not rushed into any situation he was not yet able to handle.

The owners followed my recommendation and within four days, Tiny was emerging from his corner to eat. He no longer had to be dragged out to the yard—he went willingly on his leash. Within three weeks he was using his doggy-door without fear and was reliably housetrained. At this point we began his basic obedience program, and he learned eagerly, intelligently, and quickly.

Tiny recovered as well as was possible after having experienced serious kennel syndrome. He never became an extroverted, high-spirited dog, but he was responsive, affectionate, and emotionally stable. His owners showed sensitivity and understanding in their relationship with him and saw Tiny through the hard time successfully.

Alas! Tiny never learned to bark when he heard the doorbell. However, when the door was opened, there sat Tiny, a full-grown, rather large Rottweiler—he was deterrent enough!

Lack of socialization creates a great variety of fears (fear of children, of men, or women, of other animals, of yards, of indoors, and so on). Some of these are dangerous fears and can push a dog over the edge into overt aggressive or fear-biting behavior. In Ebony's case such insurmountable fears could not be helped as long as she was in the home of the people who adopted her. Her only hope was a different environment where the humans had the time, patience, willingness, and secure emotional conditions to rehabilitate her and make her life as normal as possible.

CASE OF THE TERRIFIED DOBERMAN

Ebony was an eleven-month-old spayed female Doberman who was adopted by a family consisting of a husband, a wife, a fourteen-month-old child, two Yorkshire Terriers, one cat, and five birds in as many cages around the house. The husband was apprehensive of Ebony because of the behavior she displayed.

Biting Caused by Fear

Finally, let's look at the fear-biter. The most important thing to remember is that any, and I do mean *any*, dog can be made into a fear-biter regardless of breed, size, sex, or age. The most frequent incidents in this area are dogs who bite when cornered, trapped, repeatedly hit by a person, or harassed by children. The fear bite is usually a quick puncture, what I describe as an in-and-out bite (as opposed to tearing and ripping), after which the dog will escape the area. He will also exhibit submission and regret by licking the very hand or arm he nailed.

To elicit the fear bite, it is essential that the dog has *no avenue of escape*. This is true of all animals, including the human animal! We would much rather avoid violent confrontation if at all possible, thus it is eminently sensible to avoid placing the dog in a position where his only recourse, when frightened or cornered, is to bite. Give him the possibility to avoid the fearful situation and he will do so.

This is a problem I encounter most often with dogs who live in a home with toddlers. (Read Chapter 6, especially if there are toddlers or young children in the home.) Amazingly, once you understand the causes for fear bites, you will be far more willing to put in some supervision of the child and forestall any such incidents. By the time the child is running and walking steadily, he should be trained in kindness and the light touch, and the dog who has been mistreated will revert willingly to his devoted and loving self. Otherwise, if a child is allowed to practice abuse toward an animal without consequences of such behavior, I consider it a tragedy waiting to happen. The child who is allowed to get away with cruelty toward a helpless animal may develop serious and dangerous problems later in life.

During the day Ebony was left in the yard alone where she barked plaintively. When approached, she would show terror, and the only way to get her inside was to herd her from two directions. Once in the house, she would go into a corner, lie flat on her stomach with legs splayed, body rigid, tail down, and ears flat, giving the eye to anyone who came near. If touched, she jerked with fright so overwhelming that it seemed to paralyze her—she could not even back away. Ebony was unreachable, let alone teachable, in this condition.

Ebony's background: She was the offspring of a pregnant mother who was rescued from the pound in the late stages of pregnancy by a veterinary hospital employee. Of her rather large litter, four pups survived, and because of various transitional circumstances, they were never socialized. Although healthy, they displayed all the classic symptoms of nonsocialization. In fact, one little female was euthanized when her condition showed such difficulties that could only be described as a complete mental and emotional breakdown. Ebony was merely passed from home to home when no one proved able to cope with her difficulties. The present owners only called for help when she growled at the husband.

When I asked why they wanted a Doberman in the first place, the wife said that *she* wanted a dog to be with her in her shop for protection during business hours. Ebony was certainly a poor candidate for such a career. Neither owner had time to make the commitment to undertake an involved program, and they were beginning to be afraid of her. It was determined during the lengthy consultation that Ebony could not respond to any attempts on their part. While socialization is possible even at her age, it would have required the kind of effort they were not willing to make.

Therefore, I recommended that she be re-homed with people who were able and willing to give the involvement needed, who would work with her and who would be dedicated to change her life. Fortunately, Ebony found such a home with a young man who had the willingness, commitment, and tenacity to work with the young dog consistently and patiently.

When I last saw Ebony at the age of 18 months, she was a different dog. Her fear had abated, her eyes sparkled, her coat was sleek and shiny. Although she was cautious and a little wary, her behavior pointed to a rehabilitated, stable, and balanced animal.

Fear turns easily into aggression. Often a dog will behave in an ambivalent manner, acting fearful and aggressive at the same time. To make things even more complicated, his tail will probably wag like a metronome. I see this often when a pool cleaning person enters the backyard carrying long poles and strange equipment. This is scary for the dog and he will retreat (flight), stand and stare (freeze), or will attempt to attack the equipment and whoever is carrying it (fight). Many times, in a predominantly white neighborhood a dog will bark at a black person, and in a predominantly black neighborhood he will bark at a white passerby. Many people believe—erroneously—that the dog has been trained to do this. Not so! The fact is that the dog lacking socialization is simply not used to seeing humans who look drastically different from those he is used to.

If the situation is correctly handled, the dog will get over such fears and accept almost anyone, regardless of color or appearance. Especially if the object of his fear is calm and is willing to allow the dog to approach (*always* with the owner present) and make friends. By the way, remember that wagging tail? Well, forget it! That is not the end of the dog that will bite! Watch the face, the mouth, the ears, and the total body language!

CHAPTER

9

Warrior Dogs

The one thing nearly as horrifying as an attack on a person by a dog is a serious fight between two or more dogs. Most people are quick to act by a) trying to separate them by hand, b) beating them with any-thing within reach, c) turning the garden hose on the fighters, or d) yelling at them in the hope that they will pay attention.

When dogs fight, the sight is truly frightening, and the observers usually end up shaken. In fact, the people around should have strong and healthy hearts because the spectacle has on occasion caused heart attacks in owners and bystanders. Two ordinarily tame and benign, affectionate beings turn into savages who can inflict considerable damage on each other. The sounds accompanying a serious dogfight are bone chilling!

Attempts to separate the fighters invariably result in injury to the one who is making the attempt—not because the dogs mean to hurt the hand, but because when they fight, dogs will clamp down on a*nything*. If your hand is within reach, so be it. Yelling at them or beating them is utterly useless because in the process of the fight, they are literally anaesthetized to any outside sensation or interference. The garden hose and water may work once or twice, but if it does not, you will still be helpless in your attempt to separate them.

If you have two fighters and you are not alone, your best bet is the tail-lift. Both you and the other person grab a tail and lift each dog until the hind feet are off the ground. Once such traction is removed, the chances of the fight coming to an end are much better. Be careful to keep holding the tails and feet high until the combatants calm down and stop to take a breath, otherwise they may turn and snap at your hand. If your dog does not have a tail, then grab the hind legs and lift them, again removing traction with caution.

Dogs fight for survival. They do not fight for money or material possessions. They fight for leadership, territory, food, physical and emotional security, relationships, and defense of themselves, their young or their families— both human and canine. Dogs are usually not bullies, but there are times when physical separation is the only answer.

A few words of wisdom: if you decide to add two or three companions to your home and hearth, do your best *not to get more than one female*. Above all, *do not get sisters from the same litter.* I hear it so often that females are gentler, sweeter, more affectionate, more loving, and more intelligent. But please remember, while this may be true, one thing is certain—they are fierce fighters, and once they start fighting between themselves, you may have a serious problem on your hands. This does not mean that *all* females will fight, but the odds are better than even that they will.

It has been my experience over the years that both males and females can be loving, gentle, intelligent, sweet, protective, and affectionate. It has to do with the individual personality of the dog and the way each is treated. (What you put into the puppy is what you'll get out of the dog). But when males fight, fierce as it may be, once the hierarchy has been established, it tends to be over. If a male and a female fight, the male has a tendency to back off ("OK, lady! I get the point!"), and again, the fight is over. It is females who don't seem to be forgiving and will not stop.

CASE OF THE BULLYING BULLDOG

Gwendolyn was an eighteen-month-old spayed female Bulldog, adopted at the age of eight months into the home of an elderly couple with a nine-year-old spayed female Bulldog named Flower who had lived with her owners since she was eight weeks old. Before Gwendolyn was adopted, she went through several homes where the owners were working people and did not have the time to deal with her aggressive behavior with other animals. She did, however, adore people! When her present owners found her in the holding cage of a humane rescue group, she was emaciated, dehydrated, and in need of food. She was brought into the rescue area the day before, and more than nourishment, she seemed to crave attention and affection. The present owners' hearts went out to her and she found a home.

After several months of devoted care, Gwendolyn felt safe enough to feel at home and became a healthy, robust, and active animal. About six months before I met her, she also began to show hostility toward Flower, which gradually developed into attacks. She never injured the older dog, but when Flower would lie down in submission, Gwendolyn would hold her neck and keep her down, growling thunderously. Not a good portent for their future together! She could be pulled off each time, but help was needed here. When I arrived, the home had already been rearranged with the help of several baby gates to separate the two. Once Flower was out of her sight, Gwendolyn was back to the calm, affectionate, and playful character she was.

As I checked out the dogs, Gwendolyn appeared to be in good health. However, Flower was a little old lady, frail and delicate. Most importantly, she did not have a single tooth in her head. Over the years she had lost some, others had been extracted, and now she had a modified diet to accommodate this condition. Little was known about Gwendolyn, but the owners were able to discover that because of her color and conformation she did not qualify as a show dog. Consequently, the breeder placed her in a cage by herself at six weeks of age (rather early to determine her show qualities) and forgot about the important matter of socializing with other animals. She was not even allowed to play with her own littermates! The only interaction she had was with the humans who gave her food and water and occasionally cleaned out her enclosure. This limited but inevitable interaction was responsible for her love of people.

Gwendolyn was an alert, comprehending animal. After her repeated hostilities toward dogs in other homes, she came to this one. She realized that Flower was old, had no means of either defending herself or retaliating. In this way, Gwendolyn did indeed, become the classic little bully. And because she was an eager and affectionate soul when alone in a room without Flower, we decided to put her through brief obedience exercises daily in order to let her know that she was not the leader—the owners were.

Because of Flower's age and condition, we discussed several points: Flower could obviously not cope with Gwendolyn and it was not likely that Gwendolyn would stop her hostilities against the older dog. Apparently through her trials and tribulations, she evolved into the typical "one dog in the home" pet. Therefore, the kindest thing to do was to separate them with the help of baby gates. Each was given special time with the owners daily. They ate and slept in separate places.

This was not a solution to the problem. Because the owners were not even considering giving up either of the dogs, this became a *management* problem, which was acceptable, and the dogs lived fight-free for the next three months at which time Flower succumbed to old age and renal failure. The baby gates could be removed, Gwendolyn continued to be a good, people-loving dog, and the owners wisely did not introduce another animal into their home.

Sometimes the owner *teaches* the dogs to fight. I'm not talking about people who actually train dogs to fight each other in the pit until they are grievously injured or dead. I am talking about the unwitting teaching of dogs. Remember, *dogs imitate*. Just as it is unwise to discipline a child in the presence of other children who are then likely to imitate the grownups, it is unwise to discipline a dog in the presence of his peers for the same reason. That is what happened to poor Lily.

CASE OF THE BATTLING BOXERS

The three female Boxers who greeted me at the door were handsome show dogs, well cared for and happily inquisitive. Marlene was three, Zoe almost three, and the baby, Lily, was just one. All three were intact. About three months before, the two older dogs started to gang up on Lily "for no apparent reason." The owner seemed to be concerned more with scars and the appearance of the dogs than with the reason for the attacks. She just wanted them stopped. The lady was not exactly pouring forth information as to when, how, why, and where the attacks took place, but after an hour's relentless but tactful probing, a scenario began to take shape.

It seems that she came home one day and found a puddle on her bedroom carpet. All three dogs were reliably housetrained, so it did not occur to her that something may have caused this breach of etiquette. Instead, she looked at the dogs, pointed at the stain and demanded, "Who did this?" As bad luck would have it, Lily flinched, which "proved" to her that Lily was the culprit. The possibility never occurred to her that the pup may have flinched at the threatening tone. She proceeded to physically punish the pup in front of the other two, who were watching all this with great interest. Then she tossed all three out in the yard as punishment.

This scene was repeated again a few days later. The crime was discovered, she pointed and demanded the identity of the guilty one (did she really think they would tell?). Lily was cowering and was punished again in front of Marlene and Zoe, and then all three were exiled to the yard. After four or five such episodes, the attacks started against Lily.

It took a while to explain and convince the owner of the emotional state of her dogs, the possible reasons for breaking housetraining, and the inherent danger of punishment, especially within sight of another in the household. Merely flinching and cowering in reaction to loudness and anger is no indication, let alone proof, of guilt. And while she was unwilling to accept this,

fortunately she was concerned enough about future injuries to her show dogs to be willing to listen and agree to suggestions.

The first step was to board Lily for one week. During the week that Lily was away, the crime was committed again, and this time when she demanded to know who did it, neither Marlene nor Zoe responded. This, at least, convinced her that a) Lily was not necessarily the criminal, and b) cowering and the showing of "guilt" by an animal has little to do with what *we* determine the dog should feel guilty about. Since she now accepted these facts, she was more willing to change her other attitudes as well.

First, all three dogs were examined by their veterinarian, and Zoe was found to be suffering from cystitis. This was treated with medication and the urination inside the house stopped. Before Lily was brought home, a long discussion took place about what she called disciplining (I call it punishment) one dog in front of another. The most common problem is that the onlookers imitate the owner who does the punishing, and begin to do it themselves. Being exiled in the yard merely adds stress and frustration to the situation.

This is what happened to the three boxers. Marlene and Zoe imitated the owner, Lily was innocent of wrongdoing, and Zoe, suffering from cystitis, could not help herself. The owner, not observing carefully what was going on, literally created the fights. She was persuaded by the circumstances to start a basic obedience program for her Boxers, to learn the skills of leadership and communication herself, and teach self-control to her girls. I was able to persuade her that basic obedience would not interfere with their careers. What if they do a *sit* in the ring? Simple: teach them what the *good sit* means, and then *do not say it in the ring*!

The owner began to enjoy this new form of involvement and really got to know her animals, their different personalities, likes, idiosyncrasies and foibles—as well as her own. She began to see them not merely as show dogs but as individuals with minds and talents of their own. Realizing that she enjoyed this new relationship much more than competition, she retired the three Boxers from the show circuit and settled down to enjoy her companions.

Fortunately, the attacks on Lily stopped and never recurred. I say *fortunately*, because more often than not, once they start, they continue. But these three gentle ladies got along well and remained friends.

If two dogs live in the same household for many years in perfect harmony with never a growl between them, and a fight erupts, chances are good that it will be over food. This has nothing to do with hunger. It is merely that no matter how affectionate they are with each other, or whether they are closely related or not, food is sacrosanct, not to be touched or trifled with. The same goes for edible toys such as rawhide chewies. It is then the better part of valor to feed them as far apart from each other as possible, each in his or her own bowl, and when the food is gone, *remove the empty bowls*. Why take a chance of a fight? While they will share water willingly, food is another matter.

Sometimes fighting has a totally unrelated cause, as in the following case of Etna and Stromboli.

CASE OF THE TINY AMAZONS

Etna and Stromboli were female Italian Greyhounds. Etna was seven and Stromboli just two. There had never been any trouble between them and both became depressed when separated for any reason. About three months before I saw them, Etna attacked Stromboli "for no reason." The first time, no injuries were sustained by either dog, but in subsequent forays, Stromboli's side was punctured by Etna. Both dogs appeared to be healthy and no medical examination was done since the fights began. After each attack was over, they continued to be as friendly and devoted as before.

While observing the animals, I noticed that Etna's movements were a little hesitant. I didn't think it was related to pain or physical discomfort. It seemed more like a lack of confidence. When she would hear a sound, it was as if what she heard needed validation. She would raise her tiny chin, listen intently, and "taste" the air. Having seen this behavior, I asked the owners where the attacks occurred and when. It appeared that most of them happened in the kitchen where the intensity of light was considerably lower than in the rest of the house. I also noticed that both dogs were fed from the same, large bowl. Armed with this information, and having seen Etna's hesitancy, I decided to check her vision to the extent possible under the circumstances. Etna followed my hand well enough from a slight distance, but as I moved the hand farther, her accuracy faltered and her nervousness increased, following my hand less and less. If I jerked my hand suddenly, she would startle and rush forward to make sure that something had really moved.

I recommended that Etna be immediately examined and her eyes thoroughly checked. If it was a temporary and treatable condition, then it could be taken care of. If the condition was irreversible, then certain changes and adjustments would have to be made in the little dogs' lives to make things easier for both of them. Also, regardless of what the problem might turn out to be, each dog was to be given her own feeding dish, and they were to be placed at two opposing ends of the kitchen and removed when the food was eaten. Both pups were examined, and while Stromboli got a clean bill of health, it was found that Etna was gradually losing her sight. Her vision had deteriorated to the point where sudden movements startled her. This was the reason for the seemingly "unprovoked" attacks on the active Stromboli, especially if the younger pup accidentally collided with Etna. The owners were assured that Etna's condition and possible future blindness need not create a major upheaval. With help, Etna's life could be as happy and full as before. By creating scent signals for her, Etna would soon learn to navigate safely and Stromboli could turn out to be her best "nurse."

This was a case that I followed for a long time. Etna's sight worsened and could not be saved, but she adjusted well. The use of separate feeding dishes, never rearranging the furniture, and sound and smell substituted for her loss of vision. In the garden, Stromboli took over the job of guiding the older dog around, and she took her duties very seriously. If Etna was in danger of colliding with a tree or a bush, she would gently yip and cut off her approach to the obstacle. No attacks recurred and the two little Amazons were at peace again.

Finally, it is very important to know that fights can also erupt in a home if a new dog is brought in without proper introduction. It is easy to forget the feelings of the established dog, especially if the newcomer is a small puppy. We carry the puppy around, cuddle him, love him, and give him lots of attention. We forget that the older animal is watching these shenanigans with concern and fear of being transplanted in his owner's affections and life. Naturally, he will resent the cute and adorable intruder. The best way to proceed in such cases is to introduce the two dogs on neutral ground. Don't bring a new dog on the established dog's territory and expect him to like it. Introduce them *before* you bring the puppy into the house. The park, the puppy's home, or the street in front of the house (if the established dog does not regard it as his) will do well for this purpose.

When the new puppy sleeps—and young puppies do a lot of sleeping—give a little extra attention to the resident dog. Even when the puppy is awake, remember to feed the older one first, greet him first, pet him first, leash him first—after all, he has squatter's rights. The puppy will not suffer emotional traumas because of this, but the older dog could.

Once the fear created by the interloper is removed from the established dog's mind, he will be much more willing to accept the new pup (or kitten), be friendly, play with him, care for him, teach him, and put up with his childish pestering.

CHAPTER

10

The Exiles

Exile or isolation of a companion animal occurs when the owner doesn't want to be bothered, can't turn off what he would like to be a mechanical toy, when Chester is underfoot, or is considered to be a "yard dog," or other, innumerable reasons. Exile is dealing with the situation in the laziest possible way because all it requires is a yard, another room, a crate, or a garage. No time is spent and no effort is made to educate him to fit into the family in a way that he is truly a part of it rather than *apart* from it.

Nobody likes to be isolated. In fact, it is used as a punishment with unruly children. "Go to your room!" Haven't we all used this method of problem solving at one time or another? It may have worked temporarily, but I believe dealing with the problem itself is better than turning a room, a yard, or other specific area into a place of punishment by isolation.

Isolate Chester, who is a pack-animal, a social creature, extremely owner-oriented, and you will have some very interesting problems to deal with. Escaping, barking, digging, and hostility are just a few. Add more exotic elements to the isolation (electric shock fences, for example) and you will really have a tough time trying to overcome what you helped create.

CASE OF THE SHOCKED SAMOYED

Tanya's case was a graphic illustration of misfortunes that result because of a stubborn owner. She was a ten-month-old spayed female Samoyed who was tearing up flower beds. When I saw her, she was extremely thin, nervous, and restless, suffering from diarrhea, which was being treated but, according to the owner, was not improving.

When I looked into Tanya's physical environment I found that she was locked out in the yard for eight to ten hours during the day. There were a large number of cages stacked in the open garage containing dozens of rabbits. The entrance to the garage was blocked with chicken wire so that Tanya could see, but not go near the little critters.

Being outside and alone for long periods of time, combined with the teeming rabbits near her created a deep, unrelieved frustration in the dog. As for the physical illness, from the owner's description it had all the earmarks of colitis. Tanya was placed on a special diet and proper medication by her veterinarian, but the young woman thought the diet was "boring" and kept changing her food every few days. The medicine sat on the kitchen table, hardly used (if used at all), and she used various additives on the advice of friends, none of which were approved by Tanya's doctor. More than likely, he was not even aware that the owner was jazzing up Tanya's diet. When the owner installed electrical wiring in the flower beds, which shocked Tanya cruelly (because this woman believed that more is better), her condition worsened. She could not sit still for long, the diarrhea intensified and the weight loss continued.

I strongly recommended that the prescribed diet be strictly adhered to, the medication administered regularly as prescribed, and the fancy additives immediately discontinued. While homeopathic and herbal remedies are useful and effective, they must be monitored by an expert in the holistic field. This was not the case here.

I also suggested that Tanya be given access to a part of the house through the back door which led to the kitchen and a utility room so that she could escape the high temperatures outside and have a change of scenery. I advised the owner to spend more time with Tanya because giving her food and water—and nothing else—is unkind and leads to problems. Let her in the rest of the house under supervision and adopt a calm, peaceful attitude that the dog can sense, respond to, and feel good about. I showed the woman that with such a tranquil atmosphere, Tanya was able to relax and rest, which she did at my feet all through my visit.

She was asked to remove the electrical wires from the flower beds and until Tanya completed her basic obedience program, they should not be replanted. As for leaving Tanya alone in the house reliably, she was advised that once Tanya's education (and her own) started, she was to be left alone for short periods of time, gradually increasing the absences until she got used to the new situation and could be left alone without worry.

Tanya was receptive and an eager prospective student. This was demonstrated to the owner, but despite her dog's ability and willingness to learn she was not interested in teaching her anything because "no damn dog is going to run my life." It proved quite useless to explain that the demands we place on companion animals must be realistic ones. *Tanya could not learn theory!* As for her fears of damage in the house, the dog must be taught what is available to her and what is off limits. This cannot be taught *without* being in the house. Also, tampering with prescribed diet and medication is going to make things worse, not better.

She refused to educate Tanya but latched on to what I suggested about leaving her alone for short periods of time, combined with totally unemotional departures and arrivals, forgetting completely (or perhaps not even paying attention) that such methods work in conjunction with a program of education for Tanya. As a result, as soon as I left at the end of the consultation, she left the house for five minutes and sure enough, no damage was done. An hour later she left for ten minutes, again with success. The third time, probably using her original reasoning that "no damn dog is going to run my life," she left Tanya alone for *five hours* without knowing how to give the dog a feeling of safety and security. When she returned, Tanya had chewed a corner of the sofa. Of course, she called me saying that it was my fault because of the bad advice I gave her.

I repeated the recommendations I made over the telephone and she realized that she had missed/forgot/never heard some of what I said. Her final statement was that this was much too complicated and time consuming and that she has better things to do with her life, and Tanya will just have to "live with it." Neither her veterinarian nor I were able to convince her to reconsider, or to find Tanya a more suitable home. The owner refused because "she loved her dog."

People like Tanya's owner should never have companion animals in their care. They are not concerned with their pets' emotional (in this case also physical) well-being and stability, and they selfishly demand what their unfortunate animals cannot deliver. Isolate a dog who is unruly whenever visitors come to the house and you teach him to hate and detest anyone who enters. **Dogs are NOT stupid** and in no time at all they associate visitors with their own exile out to the yard or another room. It is only natural that Chester will dislike anyone coming to the house! It is wiser and kinder to educate him in good manners in the company of all.

While on the subject of exile/isolation, let us talk about isolating Chester from ourselves through necessity, like when we leave the house to go to work and they must stay alone for eight-plus hours. The most common symptoms of the dogs' angst are housesoiling, destruction, whining, barking, digging, chewing, and escaping. The clue that such angst exists is that these *never* occur when Chester *is not alone*.

The subject of such angst or distress of being alone is covered in Chapter 7, "The Home Wreckers." I mention it here because we are discussing not only physical but emotional exile or isolation.

Self-mutilation is a form of behavior that is often misunderstood and mishandled. It is believed that animals chew and lick themselves raw in an effort to self-destruct, as if they were suicidal. Rather, the behavior centers on survival. The most extreme form of such activity is the wild animal caught in a trap who will chew and sever his own foot in order to escape and survive. In the companion dog this form of behavior is emotional survival.

In most cases, this self-licking or chewing (acral lick) begins with a legitimate sore or wound, rash or irritation. The dog will lick and chew the spot to relieve the discomfort or soreness and this is successful temporarily, like scratching an itch. If the owner does not notice the cause for the activity, by the time it becomes apparent, the bald or bleeding spot needs extensive medical care. However, medical care alone may not be enough.

Flapjack had a good home, good food, good medical care—everything, in fact, except emotional support and interaction. He didn't have bad owners, merely uninformed ones who never had a pet before and made no effort to learn that there is more to the human-animal partnership than merely providing the physical necessities of life.

CASE OF THE BASSET WHO WOULD SELF-DESTRUCT

Flapjack was a two-year-old intact male Basset Hound whose owners despaired about his habit of self-mutilation. This is an introverted form of behavior, the basis of which often has a physical origin, which is later compounded by boredom, loneliness, lack of attention, and emotional isolation. After repeated visits to the veterinarian, muzzles, Elizabethan collars, and so on—all of which failed—the doctor referred them to me.

Flapjack appeared to be well fed and well cared for except for the unsightly self-inflicted wounds on his lower legs. He spent his life in the yard, not educated at all, and if allowed inside, it was only as far as the kitchen. He slept alone, locked in the laundry room, and food and water were given outside regardless of the weather. No play was ever initiated with him or engaged in, and his "play bows" to invite interaction were not understood, and were therefore ignored.

The problem started with a mild flea allergy, which was treated and cleared up. The licking continued and became a substitute for toys, play, companionship, amusement, and a great attention getting device. It replaced normal, healthy forms of play and interaction. Flapjack's problem was his owners who, out of ignorance, did all the wrong things to stop the problem—just as they had done all the wrong things to initiate it.

Before I could help Flapjack, I had to help his humans. They were taught that animals have intense feelings and emotions that must be considered, and because they depend on us for such nurturing, this is an essential part of animal care. Since Bassets are gregarious and affectionate, companionship, play, and attention are vital. They began to understand that Flapjack was not just an animal but a sentient being with feelings of happiness, depression, joy, sadness, tensions and stresses, pain, the desire to please, to show love and to accept the same from his family. Above all, he had the ability to communicate, which needs to be understood by the owners. They realized themselves that the self-mutilation *was* a form of communication, a means of self-preservation, and a message sent by Flapjack.

I began the owners' and Flapjack's education. The dog proved to be an excellent student. So did the owners when it dawned on them that they were thoroughly enjoying themselves and their dog. Flapjack was taught to stay alone with good feelings. He now had toys and chewies, one of the husband's unlaundered t-shirts, and the television was left on at a low volume. Proper unemotional departures and arrivals were practiced, and he waited calmly until his people came home. After relaxing a bit, they gave of themselves and of their time. He slept at the foot of their bed now and became an avid TV watcher; his meals were given inside and in every way he became a member of the family.

Flapjack learned to earn his praise and affection by obeying a simple command (learn-to-earn), and his people learned how to praise and pet him appropriately. In a very short time, Flapjack was not only responsive and a model of good behavior but also emotionally stable, happy, and a joy to have around. How do you know when a Basset is smiling? You just do...

Graduation was a proud occasion for all. By that time the self-mutilation had stopped, the legs had healed, and the owners were so tuned in to him that in their sheer delight, they added a nine-week-old Basset lady to the household. By that time they knew how to handle just about any situation (I was on call day and night, just in case). Flapjack proudly entered into the fun of bringing up Baby Pancake who in fact, reaped the rewards of everyone's education. More successful and happier owners and two more emotionally secure, sociable, and happy Basset Hounds would be hard to find.

I was most impressed and delighted with the owners' willingness and open-mindedness in working with their dog, considering their lack of knowledge in the beginning. Because of their affection for the pup and their eagerness to help him, they learned a great deal themselves and became the real winners.

CASE OF THE MUTILATED GERMAN SHEPHERD

Anton was a handsome and regal four-year-old male German Shepherd. He chewed and licked an open sore on his front paw until it bled and required medical care. This behavior went on for about two years during which time his owners tried "everything" to stop him, ranging from medical intervention, noxious substances, plastic collars, and socks on his paws, all to no avail.

Extensive history was taken when I met Anton, and a classic situation emerged. When the behavior started, Anton had a small growth on the top of his right paw, which he licked and "worried" over. The growth was surgically removed, but he continued licking it, so it refused to heal. A second medical opinion was sought and the owners were referred to an excellent surgeon who performed laser surgery to facilitate irritation-free healing. For a while the problem seemed solved, but then Anton began the self-mutilation again.

Upon questioning as to what happened in the family's life at about the same time, it came to light that the wife's brother was in an automobile accident resulting in very serious injuries, but death did not occur until several months later. I asked the wife how she dealt with Anton during that traumatic and difficult period. She recalled that she was so involved with the tragedy that she withdrew from the animal, expending all her emotional resources in trying to cope with the heavy psychological and emotional burden of the accident. Her husband, being as supportive as he could be, also unwittingly withheld the emotional input that Anton was used to.

With such a history it was quite simple to explain Anton's bizarre behavior. While the legitimate problem with the paw elicited concern and attention, once the paw healed the self-mutilation became unnecessary. However, at the very time when Anton *knew* that this injury elicited concern and earned him attention and sympathy, something happened that suddenly eliminated both the extra care and the usual involvement he was accustomed to. He didn't know why he was suddenly bereft and shut out of his family's emotional environment, but by this time he knew how to make sure that he got attention again: keep licking and chewing the paw even if the paw bled and hurt. (Remember the wild animal in the trap?) It was so important for him to get back their love and affection (which he thought he lost) that he was not deterred by bad taste or odor on the paw and managed to find a way around collars, bandages, and socks.

As the situation was described to the owners, they remembered that, indeed, this was the scenario of the last two years. Who can blame them for what happened? Even Anton didn't blame them. He was just unhappy and used the only means at his disposal, having learned from the original reaction to his injury, to say, "Have you forgotten me? Don't you care about me any more? Don't you notice me?"

It worked very well because he got attention. Not necessarily the same kind as before, but it *was* attention! If the attention flagged because the paw improved, he knew precisely how to reawaken it by licking and chewing himself again.

The owners now understood Anton's logic and his inventive method of reminding them of his presence and continuing emotional need of them. The most important step for them was to return to the relationship as it used to be in order to make it *unnecessary* for Anton to continue the self-mutilation.

Because he indulged in the chewing and licking when he was alone, it was suggested that all emotional departures and arrivals be stopped. This made their coming and going uneventful and insignificant, more a matter of fact of daily living. Instead, daily structured play periods were started during which Anton was indulged by undivided attention from his people. This could be chasing his ball, going through obedience exercises, catching a frisbee, a romp on the beach, getting a good brushing—almost any activity he liked, as long as it was done on a direct, one-on-one basis with him. This was to be Anton's time! It was carefully pointed out that stroking him absentmindedly while watching television is not what is intended because he *will* know the difference! He was also not to be petted or fondled at all, unless he earned it first (learn-to-earn) with a simple *sit*, and on compliance he was to get a brief but happy chest rub. If he happened to be sitting when soliciting attention, then the command was *down*, followed by the same happy praise and approval.

If and when licking was observed, a sharp noise was used to distract him from the activity—a table slapped with an open hand or a book, a loud bang of some sort, anything that drew his attention from the activity would serve well.

It took about four to five weeks for the self-mutilation to stop. While the distraction was an immediate remedy, for the long term cure the earned approval and praise served as relinquishment of leadership on Anton's part. Above all, the emotional input and concentrated attention-sessions were responsible for Anton's permanent cure. The added gain was that the owners, realizing the cause of the problem, saw to it that their beloved companion was as much a focus of their affection and attention as before.

Because of the last, the attention sessions could be less regimented after a while, but by then, Anton felt secure and nurtured again. The owners found again the joy and pleasure of long walks on the beach, throwing balls, and snuggling with Anton before the fireplace on cold nights. The behavior never resumed and the paws healed.

Sometimes a dog becomes so deeply owner-oriented that just the thought of being away from him is too much. That was the case with Tinker, who developed what appeared to be a fear of flying insects.

CASE OF THE COWARDLY AIREDALE

Tinker was three years old, living in a pleasant home with his family and Belle, a four-year-old female Airedale, Tinker's best friend. Belle was spayed.

The problem was Tinker's apparent fear of the outdoors when left alone in the yard, and of flying insects when he spotted them. These symptoms were interpreted by the husband as cowardice. Tinker was shown in competition several times, and while he did not show fear in the ring, he was not too happy with the experience either. Belle on the other hand, was a much calmer animal, never showing any of the fear symptoms Tinker was suffering from.

During consultation with the owners and watching Tinker and Belle, it became clear that Tinker was not *afraid* of the outdoors, but he did have two problems: 1) he was excessively owner-oriented and hated to be isolated from them even for a few minutes; and 2) being sexually mature with no outlet (since Belle could not accommodate his need), he was also frustrated in that area. His fear of flying insects was a nervous reaction stemming from his frustrations. In every other respect, Tinker was friendly, good natured, and a great pet.

I recommended that a doggy-door be installed immediately and Tinker taught how to use it. This would give him the reassurance that he could come in at will whenever he was outside, and his feeling of isolation would abate. As for his sexual frustration, it was suggested that since they were not planning to show him any more (he never placed better than fourth), he should be neutered without delay. Considering that Belle was a constant challenge to him, regardless of her sterile condition, this would make life easier and calmer for Tinker. To be on the safe side, I asked that they have their veterinarian run a neurological work-up on Tinker to make sure that the "fear" of insects was not caused by possible psychomotor seizures, common to dogs who are "fly catchers," snapping at flies who are not there.

All recommendations were followed. The neurological work-up showed nothing wrong. Tinker learned to use the doggy-door in a matter of hours (Belle was his teacher), but a small, temporary problem developed: Tinker was so eager to use it that he forgot which was in and which was out and had a few episodes of defecating inside instead of outside. The owners were advised to ignore these accidents, clean and deodorize the spots *in secret,* and give Tinker time to settle down. Within a week the accidents stopped and both dogs were using the door happily and efficiently. Tinker ignored flying insects and his owner's pride in him was renewed.

Within a month Tinker's sexual frustrations calmed. He continued life in a physically and emotionally stable state and was a most enjoyable companion.

CASE OF THE UNHAPPY CHIHUAHUAS

Sugar and Spice were two neutered male Chihuahuas, eleven and four years of age, respectively. The two little dogs got along very well. The family had recently moved into a new home and in order to have less worry during the move, Spice was left with the daughter who lived in an apartment. When the move was completed, Spice was brought home. He became restless, overactive, and began to chew his hindquarters to a bloody mess. When the owners ran out of ideas and after several hundred dollars' worth of medical bills, they called for a consultation.

Both animals were friendly. Sugar was indoors when I arrived and Spice was locked out (reason: not to have him underfoot). I never understood why Sugar was fine, but Spice would be a problem. When I asked why they wanted to have pet dogs in the first place, the husband claimed *he* never wanted them.

According to the wife, the fault lay entirely with their daughter, who kept Spice during the move, because "she allowed him inside and let him sleep in the bedroom." Considering that the daughter lived in an *apartment*, I understood why she kept him inside, and I also saw no reason why the tiny dog should not have slept in the bedroom.

When Spice came home, he was unsettled for a few days, which is why he was tossed out and relegated to sleeping in the pool house *by himself*. Sugar, in the meantime, slept indoors, making both dogs bewildered and lonely, especially at night when they had to sleep alone, whereas until then they had shared a big, comfortable basket. Spice soon began chewing himself.

Having explained what happened here, I suggested that Spice be allowed back into the family, given a chance to settle down, and allowed to sleep with his friend again. We let him in and he was exuberant for a few minutes, then settled down next to Sugar and both decided to take a nap. I explained that both little dogs had been treated poorly and each missed his friend and the reassurance and companionship they gave each other.

The house was criss-crossed with complicated security beams activated at night. I suggested that the two little ones share the laundry room with their beds and toys and be warm and snug. Thus, they would not interfere with the security system.

The husband then voiced his opinion: "No stupid dogs are going to dictate how I should live." I informed him that neither dog was stupid, especially Spice who managed very well to convey his unhappiness. While living with animals is not, and should not be, a democracy, neither is it a totalitarian dictatorship run by either himself or the dogs, but a system of adaptation on the part of both. Finally, the family prevailed on him to give it a try. It was also pointed out that the two little dogs would stabilize each other's emotional needs, and once Spice calmed down, he would be no more underfoot than Sugar and the self-chewing would stop. And wouldn't that be worth saving the medical bills? Also a short lecture was given on the subject of toy breeds and their total unsuitability to be yard dogs. While the daughter had no choice but to keep Spice inside an apartment, his short stay with her did not cause the problem.

The husband reluctantly agreed to make the change, and the wife was happy that she could keep Spice. Before I left, Spice came to me. When I picked up the little mite and cuddled him, they were astonished how much he enjoyed the attention. I suggested that they try doing it with both dogs—everyone will get to like it.

The change of location for Spice was accomplished. He was inside with Sugar, they slept together again and the chewing stopped. He calmed down and became as amiable as Sugar once the novelty and excitement of being inside wore off.

It is a terrible mistake and disservice to a companion animal to bring him into a home where he is not wanted by *all* members of the family. The one who "didn't want the dog in the first place" will convey such attitude to the animal, and the other usually feels guilty for doing it and will either neglect the dog to please the spouse or overdo the attention and affection to compensate. Neither is good for the pet.

Emotional isolation can cause another phenomenon called *pica*. This means that the dog will ingest anything and everything within his reach, including *non-food* items. He will not merely chew them but actually swallows pebbles, stockings, balls, pens, or razor blades. (I knew a Boxer who chewed the taillight of his owner's car and swallowed the bulb inside.) The owner is concerned because his first thought is that the dog must be hungry and tends to feed him more and more. However, the quantity of the food has nothing to do with the symptom. Neither does hunger. When the dog is rushed to the animal hospital to remove a bizarre object from his intestines or stomach, the owner realizes that a unique problem exists.

Not only emotional support is needed in such cases but definite education of the dog regarding leadership. Actually, if you contemplate all that has been said and compare it to individual experience, you will realize that the human-animal relationship is at its best when leadership is clearly defined and understood. It is also at its worst when this is not determined and dealt with, and the dog is allowed to become the leader of the pack.

It is not necessary for the dog's emotional health and stability to be the leader. In fact, it is better for him when he is not. He is far happier, calmer, and more stable when he knows his limits, what is acceptable, and what is not. He is happy with routine in his life. He is calmer when he is *led, not forced* but *led, taught, and educated*. It is better for the owner if the dog is a follower—well mannered, courteous, and responsive to sensible and realistic demands.

The Backyard Dog

You see him in every community: a dog relegated and restricted to the yard, porch, or outdoor run; in effect—abandoned emotionally and socially. He is fed outside, and his water and food bowl often remain empty for hours. In winter and rain he shivers, and in summer he languishes from the heat.

Thousands of years ago when man first formed his partnership with the dog, he paid for the dog's services by sharing his food and his warm, dry cave. He also incorporated the dog into his own "pack." From that time on, the dog's surrogate pack was the human family. Although times have changed, neither man nor dog are able to abandon these basic needs.

Dogs can, of course, be forced to live outside . . . but to force this kind of lifestyle is inhumane and cruel because it goes against two basic needs and instincts—the need for a substitute pack (the human family) and the need for a safe haven (the owner's home).

The negative results of a totally outdoor lifestyle for the dog is two-sided. He can go in one of two directions: 1) he may become listless, lethargic, and emotionally deprived, or 2) he may become hyperactive, fearful, noisy, or aggressive—even vicious—when the stress of such solitary life becomes too much to bear. He is fed and watered, given a little time when visited in the yard, but the rest of the time is spent alone, yearning for companionship and emotional security.

The negative aspects for the owner are also considerable. Apart from missing the joy and comfort of the dog's companionship and losing the affection and loyalty he is capable of giving, the owner also loses the *natural* protective talent the dog develops *as a member* of the human pack.

Dogs do *not* protect backyards! They may bark at people, cats, other dogs, birds, butterflies, or falling leaves, but this is not protective behavior. This is *boredom* and an intruder can easily override it with an offering of food, or friendship.

However, if the dog has free access to the inside via a doggy-door, he will protect the house because it is his den as well. Such dogs are the best and most reliable protectors. At the same time, they are also protected from the elements, abusive strangers, and dog-nappers.

What can the owner do if confronted with an intruder? "Hold on for a moment until I get my dog"? Hardly! Would it not have been wiser to have the dog inside with him all along, where he would have warned the intruder before entry, and alert the owner at the same time?

In addition, there are a number of physical and safety-related hazards the "outdoor" dog faces: heat stroke, winter weather, insect bites, and swimming pools. My suggestion is, if you intend to do this to your dog, it's best not to get a dog at all.

Varieties of Canine Problems

T here is a great variety of problems that do not come, at least in my mind, under a generalized heading. Thus, I have presented them singly in this chapter, each as a problem of its own kind, limited only by the inventiveness of the dogs and their owners.

LIES AND BETRAYALS

Let's start with a problem that stems from you, the owner. Lying to your dog destroys his trust in you. The most glaring example of this is when I meet with an owner whose dog runs away from him and refuses to respond to the recall (because he was never taught to do so). When I ask how the owner has dealt with this in the past, the statement is almost always "I catch him, beat the heck out of him, and he still does it."

If you do this you are simply lying to your dog! You catch him, then beat him. Would *you* go willingly to someone whom you know is going to beat you the minute you get there? Then why should your dog?

The command *come* must connote something pleasant and happy for Chester. When you give the command *come*, then compliance with it must be rewarded, not punished! Maybe he took a little longer to respond than you would have liked, but remember, there are distractions galore out there! If you put aside your anger and impatience for an escape and reward your dog immediately upon his return to you, he will learn in a very short time that responding to the recall and coming to you is the most pleasurable thing in the world. In fact, even if you have to chase him and catch him, praise him and love him the moment you make contact! Do not for a moment think that the dog doesn't know what he is being praised for. He knows it is not for the running but for the return. Dogs are not stupid.

Then there is the dog who is perfectly well behaved and amiable, but there are times when you reach for him and he snarls or bites your hand. This is a mystery to you because he is not vicious, and on the whole, he is a good dog.

This is almost always the result of the owner who wishes to punish his dog for some infraction and coaxes the dog to come to him. When the dog comes near, the owner pounces and zaps the dog with physical punishment. *This is pure betrayal!* Naturally, after a few times of this, the dog will not only refuse to come, but will hide under the bed, the china cabinet, the desk, or anywhere possible.

What does the owner do? He goes up to the dog and reaches in, pulls him out, and proceeds to zap him with physical punishment! Clever and effective, right? Wrong! Because, again, the owner forgot that his dog is not stupid. In no time at all, the dog learns that the reaching hand means pain and fright, and he will lash out at the hand that hurt him. Now the owner feels betrayed because all he wanted to do was to stroke his dog, except that to the dog the reaching hand is now a dangerous threat. Clever pup!!!

Rule #1: Never call your dog to you and then punish him. If you must admonish or distract him, go *to* him.

Rule #2: Correction is necessary. *Correction* means that Chester's unacceptable behavior must be changed *when it happens so that he can make the connection. There should be no such thing as delayed punishment.*

Rule #3: Punishment is unacceptable. For one thing, it doesn't work! In order to have Chester behave the way you would like him to, he has to be motivated. The best motivation I know is reward (enthusiastic praise), positive reinforcement for the kind of behavior you are looking for. (Praise good behavior even when you did not ask him to do a certain thing but he does it anyway). Punishment is fraught with danger. Hit a dog enough times and he will justifiably develop a fear of hands, rolled up newspapers, raised arms, and a fear of *you.*

The time will come when he decides that he's had enough! The next logical step he takes is retaliation. Now he is going to give you a taste of what you've been doing to him. The only way he can accomplish this is with two powerful jaws and lightning speed. He bites you! Was he justified? You bet he was! You taught him self-defense!

The worst danger is that if you have children in your home, they learn from you. They imitate you when they see you hitting the dog. After all, if Dad beats the dog, or Mom slaps him in the face, it must be the right thing to do. When he retaliates against the child, you are even more convinced that Chester is vicious, and so you get rid of him. Chester did not learn proper conduct and neither did you, nor did you teach it to the kids. Everybody loses!

Perhaps you don't permit your kids to beat the dog. It is a privilege you reserve for yourself. However, the kids don't have to *beat* Chester to risk retaliation. All a child may do is lift her arm to throw a ball, wave, dance, or reach for something, and the dog sees the raised arm as a threat or the signal that it may descend heavily on him. So he reacts the way he has been trained by you.

But you say that you reward him when he is good and only beat him when he is "bad." Great! Now Chester is getting attention for both good and bad behavior. Don't subject a companion animal to such confusion—therein lies the path to mental illness.

Do *not* equate discipline with punishment. The former is *a way of life* with limits and parameters. The latter is physical intrusion and intervention. Remember: punishment *stops* unwanted behavior for the moment, but discipline and education *changes* unwanted behavior for life.

THE WIZARDS OF OHMS

NOTE: Again, the following is not an inherent "dog problem," but the use of electricity to control dogs can have very serious consequences.

In the field of animal behavior, as in any other profession, it is vital to keep up with new developments and studies. Recently I have noticed an interesting trend: the advocacy, recommendation, authoritarian claims, aggressive marketing, and the increased use of electricity as a means to control companion animals, be they dogs, cats, ferrets, horses, and even rabbits.

Electric shock is advocated to train dogs, solve behavior problems in dogs and cats, and even regulate physical functions such as inappropriate elimination in "stubborn" animals. Nowhere do the brochures or manufacturers urge the owners to seek thorough medical evaluation before any type of behavior modification—let alone electric shock—is recommended and used. This is unethical!

It is claimed by the manufacturers and advocates of these devices that they do not hurt the animal but merely deliver a mild stimulus. However, I have yet to meet an electronic trainer who was willing to put on one of these collars and let me test it on his neck, which leads me to strongly suspect that what they call a mild stimulus is similar to calling the San Francisco earthquake a minor seismic episode. From what I have seen of these devices, I would describe their effect as more than just that. Because if it was mild ("like a tickle" said one trainer), it would certainly not stop the dog. Also, because the dog's body has a higher salt content than that of a human, the mild stimulus probably is not so mild.

When the voltage has to be increased (and it will be in cases where the dog overrides the mild stimulus), it is no longer a tickle—we can safely describe it as a shock. Whether the shock is delivered to the neck, the feet, the hip, or the rectal area (as with a prod), or to any part of the body, it becomes a cruel, painful, and horrifying experience for the animal. It is also a deep betrayal of the animal's trust, affection, and intelligence.

The side effects are not to be disregarded. The animal's reaction to electric shock is the same as that of any seriously threatening situation. He will freeze, his blood pressure and heart rate will increase, and he will startle easily (a fear-biter in the making). Electric shock is an unconditional stimulus and the reaction is a conditioned response, which takes place as rapidly as it does in humans. This consists of readily measured behavioral and psychological changes. Once the animal is conditioned in this manner, the fearful reaction is relatively permanent.

A treasure-trove of testimonials are offered by the manufacturers of such devices. The scat-mat is described as "the greatest invention since the wheel." These devices do not teach good manners or good behavior. They are also not the answer to delayed punishment, because there is no effective or useful delayed punishment.

What *is* being ignored in this frenzy of electronic danse macabre is the animal. His intelligence and ability to learn and reason are trivialized. The wizards of ohms are unwilling or *unable* to teach the owner and the animal how to deal with unwanted behavior. They also deprive both partners of enjoying life together, of interacting, of learning and teaching each other. Therefore, the advocacy and use of electric shock devices is comparable to a pediatrician using intrusive aversion techniques with a child, without examining and questioning, in great detail, the child-parent relationship.

So what if the cat hops on the counter? Cats have done that since cats came into human houses. What if the dog sits on the sofa to look out of the window? Dogs have waited for the homecoming of their humans since dogs have been invited into warm and dry caves. Why should your companion be barred from specific rooms with such hurtful methods? It is far more kind to teach him acceptable behavior in *all* the rooms in the house and not worry about having to zap him for infractions. It is simpler and less stressful for both owner and dog to cover the sofa with a pet cover (an old sheet or blanket) than to worry about policing the pet with pain and fright.

"The science of animal behavior is a relatively exact discipline since animals appear not to reason out a behavior. Instead, they function under rigid principles of inherited and learned reflexes. Thus the diagnosis, treatment, and prevention of behavioral problems can be well defined." So states the *Canadian Veterinary Journal*. Apparently they have not yet traveled far enough from Rene Descartes' opinion that *animals are merely programmed machines.* But the manufacturer uses the above quotation to justify electric shock as a means of behavior modification. Yet those of us who live and work with animals and their owners, who understand and observe them, we who take the time and effort to teach animals, know that animals *do* reason out their behavior. They *do* learn from us, not only easily but willingly. All it takes is a little time, effort, and commitment.

Electric shock collars have as many fans as the famous invisible fences. You bury the wire under the ground around the perimeter of the area you want your dog to stay in. He wears a collar that activates the wire (shocks his neck) when he comes near it or tries to cross it. This device promises to "protect your dog and keep him at home." The manufacturer does not say a word about the effect of this device in the rain on *a wet* dog. Do you want to mix water and electricity on your companion and friend? What a betrayal and how unethical!

Let us assume that the dog does not ignore the shock after repeated zaps and stays inside the "protected" area. The manufacturer does not explain that the product *won't* protect him if a *collar-free* dog comes inside the perimeter and attacks the collared dog. Nor does it protect him from dog-nappers who cross the wire, remove the collar, and take the dog. Worst of all, it does not protect your neighbor's child from wandering inside the perimeter where he could be attacked and injured by the captive dog, who may be afraid of or not like children.

The following was reported by William E. Campbell in his *Pet BehavioRx* newsletter in 1994:

"Nine-year-old Joey J. in Chester Township, Ohio, tried to pet a Rottweiler who had just busted through his invisible fence to try to attack two other boys ages 9 and 6. The dog turned on Joey, tearing off both his ears and mauling him beyond recognition. The dog's owner was babysitting the two brothers at the time and at first, she dismissed the boys' report of the attack. A second search of the area turned up Joey who nearly suffered a fatal blood loss. A report in *Animal People* (Jan/Feb. 94) states that local animal control officers of the township are unanimous in advising that buried electric fences will *not contain an aggressive dog or any dog who really wants to wander*. A reliable source states that the manufacturer of the fence settled out of court.

"Elsewhere, a Bichon Frise in the northwest was left alone behind his invisible electric fence. The owners discovered the fallacy of the so-called peace of mind offered by these devices. A neighbor's dog (without a collar) came over and killed the little dog. In the same area two shock-contained Fox Terriers were severely mauled by the neighbor's dog."

"Train" dogs by way of an electric device? Such a product may be a conditioning device, a robot-maker, or an instant result achiever, but never a teacher, never a communicator, never a way to show affection, commitment, and caring. These devices are not a way to forge a bond of friendship, loyalty, and love on the part of either party.

JEALOUSY

Do animals feel jealousy? You bet they do, and unfortunately it is too easy to evoke such emotion unwittingly. We read the gruesome headlines in the papers—"Dog Kills Baby"—with all the horrifying details. Good circulation for the papers, bad press for the dog. What they never seem to print in equal detail is *why* it happened and *how* it could have been prevented. This subject was covered in Chapter 6, which dealt with dogs and children, but let's look at jealousy toward anyone.

CASE OF THE POSSESSIVE SCOTTY

Lairdie was a three-year-old intact male Yorkshire Terrier, contented with his lot. He was emotionally stable and happy with his human, a single young lady. She worked during the day, and he adapted well to staying alone, waiting for her to come home to feed him, take him for walks, play, be given affectionate attention, and then to sleep with her on the bed. When the single lady acquired a boyfriend, trouble started.

Lairdie was standoffish with the young man and refused to approach him. Whenever any effort was made on the boyfriend's part to be sociable, Lairdie would literally turn up his tail and leave the room. When the boyfriend moved in Lairdie liked the situation even less and began to attack the man's legs until one day he succeeded in biting the intruder. A consultation was requested because the lady did not wish to give up either Lairdie or her boyfriend.

During the consultation several things were observed. Lairdie's owner had a habit of petting the little dog in the most incorrect manner possible: she would stroke his stomach and the genital area, including the penis, and when he would get a healthy erection, she thought it was "kind of cute." Also, whenever Lairdie threatened the boyfriend, she would "love him out of it."

I explained that both behaviors on *her* part were wrong. Stroking and petting a healthy, intact, sexually mature male dog in that way has the effect of sexually arousing him and leaves him without natural relief. This must stop immediately. Because of the long time this had been going on and because of Lairdie's much too frequent masturbating activities, the best procedure would be to neuter him and relieve him of sexual stress. This posed no problem for the owner, who had no intention of using him as a breeding sire anyway.

It was also explained that loving him out of it was not only ineffective, but aggravated the problem. Lairdie was convinced that attacking the young man was the right thing to do because, after all, *he was loved and praised and coddled after each attempt*. He was being rewarded! Therefore, this also had to stop immediately.

It was suggested that from now on, each time he tried to nip the young man, he was to be given an immediate obedience command such as *good sit!* and upon compliance be lavishly but briefly praised. In this manner he learned that attacks were not desirable or acceptable and would not be tolerated or rewarded. Compliance with a simple command, however, would gain him the reward of praise and good attention.

The recommendations were followed. Lairdie was neutered and weathered the surgery without ill effects. The owner's method of petting was also altered and Lairdie was stroked and petted only on his chest, neck, and ears—*when he earned it.*

Within two weeks Lairdie was considerably calmer in the boyfriend's presence. No hostility was shown, but he still raised a fuss at bedtime. He felt he was being supplanted in his owner's affections because there was another body in the bed. The young man was understanding and sympathetic to the little dog's feelings, so he outfitted a special, lavish basket for the little guy and set it in the bedroom next to the bed. Lairdie settled into it, with some reluctance at first.

At this time we also involved the boyfriend in Lairdie's rehabilitation by teaching him how to give the obedience commands and the method of praising and rewarding him for compliance. He entered into the spirit of the thing gladly and began to enjoy the little dog's intelligence and charm. Lairdie realized that his place in his owner's heart was not threatened by the presence of the young man. Six weeks after we started working together, the little Yorkie slept happily in his ornate basket in the bedroom.

Lairdie is contented with his lot, happy with his life, emotionally stable, and pleased with both his owners who later married. He is an inveterate "kisser" and generously dispenses his to both his humans.

Jealousy in animals is not reserved exclusively for humans. If you have ever brought home a new puppy to an established pet, you probably saw the jealousy one pet can have toward another. Not all established dogs welcome a newcomer with open paws! Unless correctly done, he will withdraw, sulk, stop eating, bark, housesoil, attack, or invent one or more wonderfully strange ways to express his displeasure.

The introduction of the new pet has to be carefully and intelligently made. The best place to do it is on neutral territory, not in the home that is the older dog's turf. Once they sniff and circle and get to know each other, accept each other, and stay calm in each other's presence, then they can be taken home. This is a delicate matter and must be done with patience, caution, calmness, and a jolly attitude. When you get instructions from a *knowledgeable* behavior specialist, listen carefully and ask questions. If you feel it would be helpful, have the specialist present to give a helping hand.

One client, Mr. Alford (not his real name), discussed the matter with me in careful detail. He and his wife and three-year-old child lived with two Boxers, a four-year-old intact male, Pepper, and a three-year-old spayed female, Bess. They decided to add a nine-week-old male puppy to the household, and they were advised in detail how to do it. In the three weeks between his consultation with me and Christmas (when the puppy was to arrive), he forgot a few points but did not bother to call me to refresh his memory. By March he was calling frantically because Pepper wanted to tear the puppy limb from limb every time they were in the same room. The only way they could exist was with Bess and Homer (the pup) together, sequestered in the kitchen behind a sturdy metal gate.

I asked him to relate to me step-by-step how the dogs were introduced. He told me that he brought the puppy home and they were introduced on neutral ground (the front lawn). Everything went well until he took the puppy inside. When Pepper saw him, "he went crazy."

"Whoa! Hold on for a minute! What do you mean 'when Pepper saw him?' What went on outside on the neutral ground?"

"Well, I introduced the puppy to Libby on neutral ground and there was no problem."

"Who is Libby?"

"She is our three-year-old daughter."

"Why did you introduce the puppy to your *daughter* on neutral ground? Why didn't you introduce the puppy to *Pepper* on neutral ground?"

"You didn't tell me that…"

At this point Mrs. Alford interjected that "yes, she did tell you, and I reminded you several times of what was explained to you, mentioning the fact that puppies and children take to each other much more easily."

Unfortunately, while she did remember my instructions, she was not at home when the puppy arrived and the erroneous introduction was made.

"Gee, I must have forgotten…"

He certainly did! He had kept Pepper in the backyard and when he was let in and found a new male puppy on his turf being admired and attended to and fondled and carried around, he went a little crazy. Since the situation was not handled intelligently in the first place, three months later it was a matter of great effort, time, and far more work to teach Pepper to accept Homer.

If the newcomer is a puppy, it is almost irresistible to "ooh!" and "aah!" over him. It is very hard not to lavish affection on the little one, pick him up and carry him around, show him off, and even defend him against the older dog. However, it is best that such impulses are consciously resisted. The extra attention should go to the one with squatters' rights! He is the one who feels threatened and displaced in your affection.

As for hierarchy and pecking order, let them work it out. This does not mean that you permit them to fight to the finish or tolerate bloody battles, but within reason let them establish who is boss. Sometimes it will not be the long-time resident and this may disturb your sense of justice and fair play. But if it is acceptable to the dogs, remember, it is their arrangement, not yours.

GOURMET DOGS

It is surprisingly easy to create a canine problem eater, be it a gourmet, gourmand, or a picky eater, one who will hold out for days because she happens not to like the food offered to her. The owner will usually panic into providing a different food, embarking on an elaborate food preparation scheme, or even allow the dog to eat all she wants, because after all *she needs to eat to survive*. The result can be a severely malnourished animal (because she happens to like and eat a nutritionally unsuitable food), or a blimp on tiny, disproportionate feet, gasping for every breath. In every case, the owner ends up frustrated and worried.

CASE OF THE GOURMET LHASA APSO

Mr. Jamieson called in a highly agitated state because his beloved dog, a ten-month-old Lhasa Apso was lethargic, droopy, and refused to eat. The veterinarian found nothing physically wrong and suggested that he call me. Mr. Jamieson was a retired actor, a sensitive and compassionate man who lived alone, with only Shilo as his family and companion.

By the time I met Shilo, he had also developed a habit of lying in a particular spot in the kitchen most of the day instead of the velvet sofas and chairs where he rested until recently, and began to eliminate in one of the corridors between the bedrooms.

Shilo was beautiful, groomed to the hilt, impeccable and elegant. A lot of time and attention was lavished on this little pup! Because the temperature outside was in the high 90s, he was not exactly bouncing around. He simply preferred the cool linoleum in the kitchen and found one spot in the living room where there was some breeze. Once there, he stayed.

The little dog was positively rotund! I don't mean chubby, I don't mean puppy-fat, and I don't mean pleasingly plump. Even for a ten-month-old puppy he was obese! He had a distended abdomen and rolls of fat all over him. He breathed heavily after the slightest exertion. He was in a sad shape.

The case was not merely Shilo's refusal to eat. It was a case of his refusal to eat a nutritious and sensibly rationed diet. He "insisted" on people food only—specially prepared people food—and Mr. Jamieson catered to him. The owner concocted chicken breasts, special hamburgers, pancakes with cream, oatmeal with half-and-half, turkey, ham, and shrimp, to mention a few. This was no difficulty for the lonely gentleman, and if Shilo turned up his already turned-up little nose at one dish, he immediately prepared something else. Poor Mr. Jamieson actually *taught* his dog to be a gourmet. The quantities were also excessive, and when the owner found something the little dog liked, he gave him double and triple portions to make sure that he "kept up his strength."

The serious hazards of obesity were impressed upon Mr. Jamieson and the danger of such an unbalanced diet were emphasized. Later I found that Shilo's veterinarian attempted to convince the owner of this, but he had to hear it from more than one expert before the impression was made. I explained that Shilo's lethargy and droopiness were the first symptoms and other, more serious health problems would develop soon.

By this time he was receptive to advice and a completely different diet was designed for Shilo. Absolutely no people food was to be given and from that day on a well-balanced dog food with total nutrition was recommended in controlled amounts at controlled times. If Shilo refused it, it was to be taken up in 30 minutes and not given back until the next meal time. This was done twice daily and repeated until Shilo thought better of the whole thing (got hungry enough) and started to eat what was placed before him.

Mr. Jamieson was concerned about the pup's health and possible self-starvation. I reassured him that I have yet to see a healthy dog starve himself to death deliberately when food was placed under his nose. Besides, Shilo had enough reserve to see him through a week without any danger of starvation. It would, however, act as an effective reducing diet. No treats or tidbits were permitted between meals so that the edge of his hunger was not satisfied. In addition, I warned Mr. Jamieson that it could be a few days before Shilo gave in, but that he must be strong and not surrender to this tiny tyrant.

Shilo held out; so did Mr. Jamieson. He stuck to his guns this time and followed instructions to the letter. However, he called me every day to report that the puppy still refused to eat, to ask if the dog was still safe. "Perhaps just a touch of chicken?" he'd ask me. Such comments fell on deaf ears and met with lack of sympathy and my determination not to let him crumble. On the fifth day, a triumphant Mr. Jamieson called to say that Shilo ate his morning meal with good appetite and without hesitation. Of course he did! He must have been a very hungry puppy and knew that his food (whatever it was) would disappear if he refused it again. By then Shilo was a hungry and wise pup.

Shilo has not refused his meals since then and continues to get his nutritionally balanced dog food. He lost the horrible excess weight and his little legs became visible. He is walked three times a day for exercise and toilet needs, and although he is a middle-aged gentleman now, his energy and bounce are still evident as is his good health and enjoyment of life. He still seeks out cool spots when the weather is hot, but he remembers his housetraining. Mr. Jamieson still enjoys the antics of the little dog and admitted to me that occasionally he will slip a tiny piece of chicken or turkey into Shilo's bowl. As long as it is occasional and tiny, why not?

COPROPHAGIA

 The voice on the telephone is outraged, desperate, and utterly revolted. I usually know what is coming because this is a problem that evokes great disgust and total incredulity in the owner's reaction to the problem—coprophagia.

"I'm grossed out! How awful! I give him the best food available, all the food he wants, keep his dishes spotless, and what does he do? He eats *poop!*"

My first job here is to calm the owner, sympathize with his disgust, and proceed to explain that while it is to us a disgusting thing to do, it is not uncommon that dogs will commit this crime. Good food, clean dishes, large portions have no bearing on the act that can be caused by enzyme imbalance (trypsin), temporary "puppy stuff," or a natural tendency to recycle nutrients, especially in cat poop. It can also be the result of introverted behavior that has no *physical* cause. Coprophagia is an occasional, isolated occurrence, but it *can* become habitual.

Punishment is not the answer to this problem. It will only make an already introverted dog even more so. After a thorough medical examination, if a physical cause is found, treatment and medication followed strictly according to the veterinarian's instructions will stop the activity. If, however, the dog gets a clean bill of health, then the psychological reasons for this disturbing behavior must be determined.

If we delve into the reasons for poop eating by animals, several interesting points come to light. Newborn puppies cannot eliminate their waste by themselves. For this reason, their mother must stimulate their perianal region, and unless she does so, the puppies will not survive. She will, at that time, ingest their waste to keep the nest clean. This behavior is a remnant of her wild state when she needed to eliminate the odor that predators could follow to her helpless young. Under these circumstances, eating the waste of the pups becomes a lifesaving activity on her part, and thus, much easier for us to understand and accept. This behavior is then maternal and sometimes remains with the dog, sometimes awakens later, especially if a new puppy comes into the home.

Stools contain undigested nutrients, and there are times when the dog will recycle them. This is also understandable when we consider that nature is not as wasteful as we are. This is particularly true when a dog happily ingests cat stool—a veritable delicacy for him, again for the nutrients that the cat has passed in the feces.

No matter how well we understand this, coprophagia is unsightly, disgusting, and undesirable in our dogs, who just a little while ago gave our faces loving kisses and will undoubtedly do so again. Not to mention that if the dog happens to have intestinal parasites, he will simply reinfect himself.

Stool eating as an introverted behavior is something else, again, but both causes must be addressed. As I mentioned before, if the problem is physical, your veterinarian will provide the necessary treatment and dietary adjustments as required. By following his instructions to the letter, the problem will be eliminated.

Let us look at a case of introverted coprophagia and how it was handled.

CASE OF THE INSECURE BEAGLE

Banjo was eighteen months old, an intact Beagle with a sense of humor and a fondness for visitors. During the initial consultation he was relatively calm but in need of some education in socially acceptable conduct. The arrangements were made to begin his schooling to eliminate jumping on people. Prior to my leaving, the owner asked, a bit embarrassed, if there was anything we could do about Banjo—ahem! You know!—eating his own stool.

Armed with this information, our first session dealt with minimal commands but extensive details were obtained about Banjo's diet and lifestyle. It seems that his diet was quite a bit different from the one originally described. Banjo was given more tidbits, people food, and goodies than the owner first admitted. To stop the unsightly habit, they tried cayenne pepper on the stool and meat tenderizer in the food. The problem would stop for a few days but then resume.

Banjo proved to be extremely submissive with his owners and did not have much self-confidence. This was certainly not helped by physical punishment or exile into the backyard, neither of which built up the youngster's sense of security. On the contrary, the situation evolved into a vicious cycle: Banjo would defecate, become anxious, eat the stool, get punished. Then the cycle would start again and this sequence kept repeating itself. There seemed to be no way to break the chain of events.

Banjo's progress in the basic obedience program was excellent. He proved himself receptive and retentive, enjoyed himself, and was eager to show what he could do. During the six-week program his diet was adjusted in several ways. The carbohydrate was reduced and the protein and calcium were increased. He was given calcium gluconate, B-complex, and cider vinegar was added to his food. (Such changes in a dog's diet are always done with the veterinarian's approval.) The amounts were carefully measured for his size and weight. He was fed twice a day instead of only once and he was placed on a rigid feeding schedule.

It was emphasized that the stool must be carefully monitored so that if it appeared too soft and not well formed, the amount of food should be reduced by 10 percent until this was corrected. If the stool was hard and powdery, a 10 percent increase was warranted. All people food, tidbits, and goodies were withdrawn until Banjo adjusted to the new diet because any such additions would delay his system's adaptation to the different food he was getting.

All punishment was stopped immediately. Banjo had no other disgusting habits, so this was easy to accomplish. He was given two daily sessions of quality time, one consisting of obedience practice with heavy emphasis on the learn-to-earn, and another for play, interaction, and fun.

When Banjo graduated with honors six weeks later, he was well on his way to self-confidence and excellent social behavior. The submissiveness gave way to a well-balanced emotional stability, the coprophagia stopped, and to date, five years later, did not resume. The owners' attitude completely changed regarding punishment and they are now of the opinion, as I have always been, that it does much harm and no good.

ESCAPE ARTISTS

Having to live with a canine Houdini is frustrating. When Chester escapes repeatedly—over the fence, under the fence, around the fence, and sometimes *through* the fence—the owner is really hurt. After all, look at the loving home he provided, all the good food, a warm bedroom, a big, spacious yard to play in. "Why does he do this to me?" the owner asks. The key phrase is "to me." Dogs are never spiteful. They never exact revenge. They only do what they do to achieve a result that is beneficial to them. Escaping is such a deed. The benefits to Chester are freedom to roam and seek females (if he is intact); exercise, which he may crave, by running free; and above all, relief from boredom and the loneliness of being separated, rejected, or abandoned by his pack (the family).

Neutering will reduce the search for possible mates. This surgical procedure has several other benefits as well. Dr. Thomas E. Vice, noted San Antonio veterinarian, states quite clearly that unrelieved sexual stimulation creates biological and psychological pressures.

Regular and suitable exercise will relieve much of the pent-up energy that many dogs relieve by running. This does not mean that you take your dog, as many owners do, twice around the block three times a week! This means taking time and effort, but the daily long walk and exercise will be beneficial to you, too. This also means that if you do not have the time and do not wish to make the effort, do not get a German Shorthaired Pointer, an Anatolian Sheepdog, or a Border Collie. Also forget Siberian Huskies and Malemutes. A small Yorkie might be a better pet for you. Working breeds with a high activity level will not adjust well to a life of idleness. Let's face it: Dogs need a job to be happy and the unemployment rate among our canine companions is very high!

The two main culprits that cause runaway dogs are boredom and isolation. Of course you give her a lovely home, a warm bedroom (usually yours). But what about the daytime when you are at work and she is alone? Oh, you put her in the yard because she will chew up the house or because she still housesoils occasionally? Maybe it's because you don't quite trust her.

These problems are easy to remedy. Let's address chewing, housesoiling, and lack of trust. Don't throw the baby out with the bath water! Don't throw out the dog with the problem—work out the problem and let her in! Give her a doggy-door, give her limited freedom of the house to start with, because that's where your scent is. First and foremost, educate her in reliable behavior and you won't have to worry about leaving her alone in the house.

An added but often overlooked benefit is that your home is protected. I do not believe in nor advocate exploitation of any animal. Nevertheless, dogs have an innate talent to guard and give alarm and this talent should be put to use. Chester will use this talent to protect his den but not the backyard. He may bark out there, but chances are he barks at everything and you'll never know whether he barks to alert you, repulse an intruder, in play or in fright, or to relieve boredom. However, if you have educated Chester and he has access to the inside, should anyone try to break in during your absence (or even when you are there) and hear a dog barking on the other side of the front door, they will most certainly reevaluate the situation and go elsewhere. By the way, when was the last time anyone tried to steal something in your backyard?

During a basic obedience program I usually talk myself blue in the face on the subject of allowing dogs access to the inside of the house at all times in order to protect it. In several cases I was proven right, much to my regret. About a year after two dogs graduated (living not too far from each other), there was a rash of daylight robberies in the area. The clients called, upset and angry that my pupils did not "do their duty" and what did I have to say about it? In both cases the dog was locked out in the backyard and so could not deter anyone in the house. I had repeatedly advised both owners to give the dogs access to the house. And, of course, neither dog's barking alerted anyone in the neighborhood because it's populated by working people who were not home to hear it.

To find out why a dog jumps fences or digs out under them, the most important questions are "Where?" and "When?" Does it always happen on Thursdays? What else happens on Thursdays? If the garbage is collected on Thursdays he could be following the truck for the goodies that may be falling off it. Is there a particular spot where he performs his Houdini act?

Aha! The lawn furniture is placed by the fence and all Chester has to do is get on the table, from which it is merely a hop and a jump to get over.

Never tie your dog to a tree or a post by a rope or chain on his neck. This is dangerous for the dog because you may come home to find her hanging dead by a broken neck. This is also dangerous for you if you have small children running around her. Imagine the frustration of not being able to join in the fun! When the frustration and eventual anger develops and the child gets too near, or happens to be screaming around the tied-up dog, an attack can happen. This is why disreputable attack dog schools use this method as the first lesson, to agitate dogs in this manner to bring out and teach aggressive behavior.

Finally, to deter escapes *raise the fence!* Not only raise it, but top it with a lid—an extension of about 14 to 16 inches (36 to 41 cm) wide, mounted on top of the existing fence, *tilted inward*. Unless she sprouts wings like Pegasus, chances are excellent that she won't be able to clear it and will stay where she is. (This type of fencing is used in wild animal parks and it works extremely well.) But she digs her way out under the fence, you say. Then sink some cement bricks at the base of the fence, also about a foot deep, which she cannot dig through.

High, sturdy fences and doggy-doors are the best tools to ward against dogs escaping. Involvement with your dog when you are at home is the best answer. Teach her the learn-to-earn, establish your leadership, and make her *want to stay home*. If there are reasons for not allowing her in the house, deal with those first, then the escaping will be a lot easier to rectify and stop.

DEAFNESS

When most of us find that a dog was born with a physical handicap, we tend to be sympathetic and exhibit pity. What we don't seem to realize is that an animal who never had a certain faculty will never miss it. No one is there to explain to him that he is handicapped, limited, or different—he just takes it for granted and nature helps him to compensate. Our job is to make sure that his safety is not jeopardized because of the handicap.

CASE OF THE WHITE GREAT DANE

Alba was about ten weeks old when she was adopted. She was snow white with blue eyes and was born completely deaf. Had it not been for the couple who fell in love with her and adopted her, she would have been destroyed. But she snuggled in their arms, licked their faces, and they were "goners." They could not abide the thought of having her killed, and in spite of the difficulties they knew they were facing, took her into their hearts and home. She was not going to be bred, and thus, she was in a safe place. Another potential problem was the couple's two existing Great Danes: Isis, the gentle and dignified seven year old, and Theodore, a two year old, unusually large youngster, full of energy and youthful fun.

It was difficult to adjust to Alba's inability to hear because one unconsciously uses voice to teach. Housetraining was easy because Isis and Theodore were not only gentle and affectionate toward the puppy, they were also excellent, natural teachers.

The problem of communicating with Alba was solved, after much thought, by sewing several small bags and filling them with beans, rice, and small pebbles so that we had several bags of differing sizes and weights.

In order to get her attention, we tossed one of the little bags at Alba's rump. The moment she looked at us, broad hand and arm signals were used to convey a command. If the owners used their voices it was fine, because although Alba could not hear them, they felt unconstrained and more natural. When Alba responded and came, she was lavishly praised by petting. Here, facial expressions were of great help because wide smiles were understood by her. The *sit* command was taught by standing beside her, leaning slightly back, and raising a hand over her head. As she followed the hand and sat, we gently petted her hips and praised her immediately. In no time at all, Alba sat by just a gentle upsweep of a hand in front of her face. In fact, to call Alba when the owners were out of sight, jumping up and down or hitting the floor created enough vibrations that Alba felt and went in search of their source. Praise and smiles—success!

Each obedience command was taught with the help of a small bean or rice bag, hand signals and happy petting for Alba's compliance. The pleasure of the owners at each step of her progress was pure delight, and Alba's learning became a source of fun and pride to them.

Isis and Theodore proved invaluable in the relationship of Alba with the whole family. Since little bags only fly so far, if Alba was too far to call with their help, Isis and Theodore would actually herd the little one toward the owners, or the door, when it was time to come in. It was Isis who provided most of the housetraining education and Theodore looked after Alba's safety and well-being.

After the six-week basic obedience program was completed, Alba graduated with flying colors. Her owners graduated with honors and earned my respect for their commitment, dedication, patience, and the loving determination they showed in living with a handicapped animal. Alba became as well educated and controlled as any hearing dog. Several little bags are regularly worn out and have to be replaced. She is now a little over 100 pounds (45 kg), a beautiful dog, with an appealing personality and joie de vivre.

There are some cast-iron restrictions for Alba, and constant management and vigilance are absolutely required. For instance, she is allowed through the front door only on a leash with one of her owners on the other end. She is not allowed anywhere without it because there may be a chance of wandering away or getting in the way of a car that she would never hear.

Alba never learned to bark, perhaps because she never heard barking, but Alba sings! Her humming voice is a source of pleasure to her family and seems to be a very effective method of communication with both her human and canine family.

Why did Alba's family go through such efforts with her instead of acquiring a hearing animal? This was their choice and their decision. Alba found a place in their hearts. They adopted her out of pity and concern, but it did not stop there. They were willing to accept the responsibility and hard work it took to socialize and educate her to function as if there were nothing wrong with her. As far as Alba is concerned there *is* nothing wrong with her! She is oblivious to her handicap, which did not affect her intelligence, energy, learning ability, or affectionate, gentle nature.

BLINDNESS

A birth defect such as Alba's is something a dog is not aware of and never misses. When the impairment develops gradually in an animal, the owners have a tendency to identify strongly with the pet and consider euthanasia, perhaps reasoning that, "if I ever lost *my* sight, I wouldn't want to go on living." This is not the case with animals, as Oedipus proved.

CASE OF THE BLIND GOLDEN RETRIEVER

It was a perversity of fate that Oedipus lost his sight and was blind by the age of six. He was an affectionate Golden Retriever who had courage and a great sense of humor. While his owners loved him dearly, they almost decided on euthanasia to prevent his suffering as a result of this tragedy.

Because he was healthy and strong, the family's veterinarian persuaded them to call me and consult on the possibility of changing their minds as well as the dog's physical environment, so that instead of killing a healthy animal, his life could be made as happy and trouble free as possible.

It would have been a great pity to destroy Oedipus! Having seen him with his loving family, it was not too difficult to persuade them that dogs adjust to poor eyesight and blindness with little difficulty and that their hearing and sense of smell grow even more acute and become directional indicators. They may stumble occasionally at first, or walk into a piece of furniture, but such mishaps can be avoided with some changes and sensory aids introduced into the dog's physical environment, and some adjustment in the human partners' attitude toward the handicapped pet.

In order to make use of Oedipus' sense of smell, we sprayed a light cologne inside the home on such objects as table and chair legs, doors, chests of drawers, and kitchen cabinets. In a very short time Oedipus learned to detect this particular scent and associated it with *"danger—obstacle ahead."* Thus he avoided the articles marked in this manner.

A different scent was used to mark the path leading to the doggy-door and the outside steps. Oedipus learned to follow a different scent for his toilet needs and for visits into the yard, and then find his way back to the door and into the house again.

To utilize his acute hearing, the family learned to call him all the time, and by their voice, identify themselves so that Oedipus knew who was with him. In addition, each family member began wearing a piece of noisy jewelry, such as a charm bracelet or small bell on a belt or a shoe. Such an item was furnished for each visitor, and Oedipus learned quickly to follow their movements with great accuracy and self-assurance. He could even find a scented ball, so that his play and fun were not lost.

The family was finally convinced that Oedipus did not suffer and need not be treated as a feeble invalid. His blindness was not to be emphasized and catered to as a handicap because this could easily undermine his self-reliance and emotional stability. Other than the recommended allowance for the absence of his sight, Oedipus was to be treated, exercised, walked, and played with as before. He was never, under any circumstances, allowed outside without a leash since he could not follow his owners' movements as precisely as before. The location and the pace of the owner on the other end of the leash was reinforced by the sound of the bracelet or little bell, as well as by voice.

My recommendations were followed and the modifications in the house were made. Oedipus adjusted to his new condition and environment with ease, speed, and a minimum of accidents or frustration to himself. His family treats him with understanding and affection; he is not babied or spoiled. They are happy that a way of life was developed for all of them so that they could continue to live an enjoyable life with Oedipus.

Note: Had Oedipus had a companion dog, the chances of the other, sighted dog taking on the job of guide were excellent. It is not uncommon, and I have seen it repeatedly, that when one of the friends becomes blind, the other will gently herd him in the right directions. It is a wonderful example of kindness and generosity exchanged between animals.

Thus we see that physical limitations are perceived differently by our pets. My beloved Nefer came to me from a dreadfully abusive situation and was lame on her left hind leg. While it was heartbreaking for all to see her limp and bob markedly, when she ran the limp was unnoticeable and her speed was not impaired. She was, however, not above using her limp on occasion, to solicit sympathy from my friends who had just met her, until I tricked her into streaking past the well-meaning persons, thus proving that pity and *misplaced* compassion were not necessary for Nefer's well-being.

Many dogs lose a leg through accidents, being caught in traps in the country, bone cancer, and so on, when amputation is the only recourse to saving their lives. The fast compensation and adjustment they are capable of is amazing and they teach a lesson in overcoming limitations. It looks sad and tragic when they hobble along, but they are not aware of it. They just go on living the good life.

BACK INJURIES AND PAIN

Some breeds tend to develop back problems more than others. Large dogs are more apt to be plagued by dysplasia of the hips, but small breeds are not exempt from trouble. The long and lean Dachshund is prone to slipped discs, West Highland Terriers can develop Perthes-Legge disease, and other small ones develop different problems in the neck area. Such was Laurie's case.

CASE OF THE TIRED CAIRN TERRIER

Laurie was a two-year-old spayed female Cairn Terrier who was a lively, active, healthy little dog until about three weeks before I saw her. Then she began to be listless, tired, refused to use the same stairs she loved to race up and down on, and was unwilling to jump on her favorite chair. At times, even walking seemed too much for her. The owners, two brothers—physicians themselves—called for a consultation when a former client suggested that I evaluate the little dog's behavior.

When I saw Laurie she looked tired, walked with cautious steps, and seemed to have difficulties moving about. In fact, she moved more like a fifteen-year-old rather than a two-year-old youngster. When she came in from the patio and had to cross a half-inch step, she hesitated, alternating

her front feet as if she wasn't sure which to use, and then very gingerly, she stepped inside. It was the way she held her head, slightly askance, not daring or not being able to look where she was going that alerted me that there might be something more involved than merely a behavior problem.

My first suggestion was to take Laurie immediately for a medical checkup with emphasis on X-rays of the complete skeletal structure as well as complete examination of the ears in case the problem was a loss of equilibrium. Two days later I received two calls—one from the veterinarian saying that my suspicion was well-founded—the X-ray showed an injured disc in the cervical area. This is what caused the inability to move freely and it also caused considerably pain. The brothers also called, delighted that the cause of the problem was discovered and that surgical procedure would correct the little dog's condition.

Three days later Laurie was operated on. Four weeks later when I saw her again, she was streaking past me, up and down the stairs, around the pool, hopping onto her favorite chair, showing me all the things she could do again, pain-free and lively as ever. Trying to get her to rest was a little difficult, but it did not seem to cause additional problems.

It appears that often a behavior problem is not a behavior problem at all. Quite often, housesoiling after years of perfect control is caused by urinary problems. Incessant chewing could be the result of hunger in the case of fast-growing puppies or dental problems in adult dogs, overactivity due to insufficient protein in the diet or allergic reaction to dyes and preservatives in the food, or self-mutilation caused by an imbedded foxtail. Therefore, the first recommendation I make to a client, before I observe and evaluate the dog, is to have him checked and examined by the veterinarian, because if the problem has a medical basis, attempting to deal with the behavior would merely add stress to the existing stress.

It is always a pleasure to discover that the problem experienced by an animal is correctable. True, it is not easy for an owner to discover hidden medical problems, but if he will studiously acquaint himself with his pet's normal behavior and mien, he can usually detect (if he notices a change) that something is wrong and seek help.

PROTEIN DEFICIENCY

The proper diet is crucial to your puppy's physical as well as emotional well-being. Certain deficiencies can lead to behavioral problems, as we see in the case of Folly.

CASE OF THE RESTLESS COCKAPOO

Folly was an eighteen-month-old Cockapoo, a well-cared-for little dog, beloved by her family composed of a couple with two children. She was a pet shop purchase with an unknown background. At first she was a cheerful and pleasant companion, but she started exhibiting nervousness about six months before I saw her.

For no *apparent* reason, her personality changed. She became restless, easily startled, barked too much at any movement and all people, including the family, and once she stopped, she would start again as soon as anyone made a move, even if unrelated to her. Entertaining guests became difficult to impossible, and the children's friends became reluctant to visit because of the clamor and chaos she created. They called for help at the suggestion of their veterinarian who, by the way, had not seen Folly for months.

Folly raised an unearthly din when I arrived. She approached, then darted back, circled and raced around, barking all the time. After about 15 minutes (during which time I always ask the owners not to correct the behavior to enable me to observe it unchecked), she finally settled with the husband, somewhat tired. The moment I would move an arm or shift my position, she would start again. My impression was that she was doing this compulsively, rather than willingly. These episodes were repeated several more times during my visit.

After getting her history, we covered her diet and eating habits. Folly was started on a nutritionally complete food, however, less than a year before the owners had begun experimenting with a variety of foods, responding to television commercials and bright packages on display at the supermarket. After several bouts with diarrhea, they settled on a commercial brand canned food that was not considered one of the better ones. Having looked at the list of ingredients on the can, I discovered that the protein content was too low. Folly was not given any supplements or dry food. Although she did not get any people food, they did feed her a full 12-ounce (373 g) can daily and she was gaining weight. Because of her recent behavior it was difficult to take her for walks.

Before dealing with the heightened nervousness and activity level, I recommended certain changes in her diet. Rather than make a complete change at this time, it was suggested that a carefully calculated amount of protein be added to her food, reducing the canned food by the same amount. In this case we used soft-cooked chicken and ascertained that no bones were accidentally left in the meat.

In addition, with the approval of the veterinarian, Folly was given daily doses of vitamin B-complex and niacinamide, which were crushed and added to her food. The new diet regime was started without delay. In two weeks the change in Folly was dramatic. She still barked at all comers but now it was a friendly "hello" lasting a few seconds, after which she settled down to a calm surveillance of what went on around her. People could move about the house again without the risk of outbursts on her part. The family had dinner parties again and invited friends who had refused to come to the house before. Folly was now a gracious and pleasant cohostess, which prompted some of the guests to suggest that I "switched dogs" on them.

I gave Folly's owners more dietary information on the undesirability of experimenting with a pup's food. This not only creates a finicky eater, but she can also insist on a food that is totally inappropriate for growth, health, and general well-being. This is what happened to Folly.

Finally, it was time now to make one last change in the little Cockapoo's diet, to a high-quality, balanced kibble in addition to the chicken and the vitamin supplements. Gradually the chicken and the vitamins were eliminated and Folly's behavior remained calm and sweet, and she lost much of the unhealthy excess weight she had been carrying around. Then it was easy to teach her courteous obedience. In a very short time Folly became the undisputed favorite of the family's circle of friends who now vied with each other for the privilege of dog-sitting when needed. The nerve-racking displays never surfaced again.

Folly was suffering from protein deficiency, insufficient calcium and the unsettling reaction to coloring and preservatives in her food. We often suffer from these additives ourselves and this has been markedly noticed in children. The B-complex and niacinamide was a balanced supplement and worked as what veterinarian William E. Campbell calls behavior insurance. However, such supplements must be contemplated *only after discussion with the veterinarian*. The doctor is able to inform the behavior specialist of the dog's general health (particularly the kidneys), and he or she will either give the go-ahead or recommend that it should not be used for medical reasons. Drastic changes or additions to a dog's diet should be made *only* with the veterinarian's knowledge and approval.

HEALTH-RELATED BEHAVIOR PROBLEMS

 Too often physical or medical conditions that the owner is not aware of in companion animals contribute to behavior problems. Sudden unexplainable urination may be caused by cystitis or stones in the kidney or bladder. Extreme sensitivity of an infected ear or a thorn in a paw may provoke a growl, a nip, or even a bite to an uninformed, careless, or even affectionately petting hand, or a hand that tries to help. Medical conditions can cause aggressive response (occipital aplasia, hydrocephalus, hypothyroidism), fearfulness, reclusiveness, or even highly agitated behavior (as in hyperkinesis). Be alert for abrupt changes in personality that may accompany illness.

Medical conditions involving the skeletal structure, particularly the spine, are often undetected by the owner. In many dogs spinal conditions will not cause behavior changes especially if the abnormality does not cause pain. In cases where the problem is painful, the owner will be aware of lameness, difficulty moving, whimpers, unwillingness or the inability to walk. In larger breeds, conditions in older dogs such as cauda equina syndrome can be so severe that the dog is unable to squat to urinate or defecate. Even a loving pat by the owner of the affected area may elicit a snap or a painful bite.

Degenerative myelopathy, which is a progressive demylineation of the motor and sensory neural tracts in the thoracic segment of the spinal cord, shows up initially in loss of procioception (sense of limb and joint position), which results in knuckling rear feet (toe-over) and progresses to inability to walk without swaying from side to side. The dog may even collapse at the rear quarters. In itself, this is not a painful condition, but in larger breeds it often occurs simultaneously with degenerative joint disease of the spine or hips, and makes an otherwise tolerable arthritis excruciating and unbearable.

According to Anders Hallgren of Sweden (*Animal Behavior Society Newsletter*, July 1992), back problems were found in 63 percent of 400 dogs examined. These problems were distributed as follows: 27 percent cervical, 67 percent thoracic, 72 percent lumbar—including the tail. Because several dogs had abnormalities in more than one location, the numbers were closer to 100 percent. There were no significant differences between females and males, and it appears that a larger percentage of dogs with spinal problems exhibited problem behavior than those without. Fear and stress were also exhibited but not in as many dogs.

Several factors can contribute to spinal problems. For example, dogs who go lame during growth because of sprains, fractures, paw injuries, or panosteitis develop back problems in larger numbers than those who do not. While the lameness may be of short visible duration, the compensation during the presence of the pain changes the posture and can create the problem.

More than 70 percent of dogs who have been in violent accidents (falls, collision with a car, fights, rough wrestling with humans, thrown about inside a vehicle, shaken as a training method) have spinal difficulties. Stretched or torn muscles can also dispose the dog for later back troubles. Seat belts, appropriate harnesses (not collars) in truck beds, caution in the mode of play, vigilance to avoid fights, and using sensible, humane training methods are the ways to avoid spinal problems.

One of the serious culprits in causing spinal anomalies is the jerking and tugging of leashes by trainers and owners. Dogs who pull and strain at the end of a leash develop back trouble far more often than those who do not.

Whiplash from such jerking is quite common, and the risk increases when a chain is used to choke the dog. This device, incorrectly used, is dangerous because pulling on it causes pressure around the animal's neck. The muscles that would absorb this kind of trauma are on the *sides* of the neck. Thus the neck itself and the throat are unprotected. Jerking on a choke chain or a pronged collar as a means of controlling a dog—and even hanging him by the neck—has been used for decades by trainers. There is a definite connection between the severity of the jerk and the severity of the damage. I have had the misfortune of observing paralysis in dogs who have been handled in this manner.

Securing the dog to a rigid object (post, fence, tree) on a choke chain and leash or rope can also cause spinal injury. The dog (especially a young animal) will forget the length of the tether, will try to take off and be jerked back suddenly and violently. The shock is then absorbed by the neck.

A small percentage of dogs who walk only on concrete or pavement or who race up and down stairs also showed some problems, whereas those who also walk on hilly terrain did not.

Finally, one more condition will place great stress on the spine of the dog: obesity. This problem is common in low-slung, long-backed dogs (Bassets and Dachshunds, for example), but regardless of the breed, obesity is not only hard on the cardiac and pulmonary systems, it also places great burden and stress on the skeletal structure, particularly the joints. This is also one of the most difficult situations to deal with because too many owners equate love with overfeeding or giving their companions inappropriate food and treats.

Exercise should be approached as humans do—warming up the muscles slowly to start. Running with dogs under the age of one and a half years is not recommended. Walking is good! Caution must be observed when small dogs play enthusiastically with larger breeds.

Sometimes the behavior problem is so blatantly related to the humans in the home that a family counselor may be needed to solve the problem, as in this next case.

CASE OF THE HYSTERICAL FAMILY

The family consisted of a mother, father, daughter, daughter's boyfriend, and a handsome, one-year-old intact male Doberman named Oscar. Reason for the consultation: Oscar was "stubborn," barked a lot, had the tendency to jump on people and was generally uncontrollable. The consultation lasted over two hours and the situation could only be described in one word: disastrous! Except that the disaster was not Oscar but the people around him.

Oscar met me happily at the door and within minutes he was friendly, interested, sniffing busily to get to know me. He did not jump on me or anyone else while I was there, which does not mean that he never did. In fact, Mother showed me some slight scratches on her arm where she collided with his paw during one of his inappropriately affectionate moments.

Oscar was intelligent, went through training class before I saw him, and was highly sensitive—and therein lay the problem. He was made extremely restless and nervous by the people around him. He was never addressed in any way except with screams, impatience, irritability, and anger because when given a command, it took him at least four to five seconds to comply. The commands usually went something like, *Come here sweetheart, sit for me, there's a boy.* And when Oscar looked at the person somewhat perplexed (especially if the command included both *come* and *sit*), the next command was *Damn you, you stupid dog, I said come/sit or else!* At this point Oscar usually departed the scene. Wouldn't you? Boyfriend would then grab the choke chain, wrestle him to the floor, hitting and yelling in the process. Oscar would howl in fright and then manage to get away. Boyfriend would follow him, trying to hit or kick him, occasionally with success.

At this point, Daughter followed Boyfriend screaming at him to leave the dog alone. Mother screamed at both to cut it out, leave Oscar and each other alone, while Father looked on quietly, at a loss. No wonder Oscar liked to be with Father more than with anyone else! And no wonder that within 30 minutes I had a dandy headache.

When everyone calmed down and seemed willing to listen, I proceeded to demonstrate that Oscar *did* respond to commands correctly given. I explained and demonstrated that a command must be clear and concise: *Oscar, come!* or *Oscar, sit!*, and then the dog was to be praised for compliance.

Oscar performed like a trouper, eagerly and faultlessly. When Boyfriend tried it, he went back to the old way and again started to scream at the hapless dog.

Boyfriend was eighteen years old going on six. He was irresponsible, out of work, a user and exploiter of people. This is only relevant because his relationship was the same with Oscar. He did not work with him, had no patience for him, no compassion, no understanding, and above all, refused to think. He stated that he was tired of the dog and had had it with him. He refused to feed, exercise, clean up after, or interact with Oscar. The only attention the dog received from him was verbal and physical abuse. So far, Oscar showed infinitely more patience and tolerance toward him than he showed Oscar!

My question was, "Who owns and has control of Oscar and who makes the decisions for his welfare?" The dog belonged to Daughter, a gift from Boyfriend. I tried to communicate with her because she seemed more willing to listen. However, as soon as she seemed to agree with me, Boyfriend would break in with, "Who the hell do you think you are, coming in here telling me what to do?" This challenge was taken up by Mother who informed him that this was *her* home, it was *she* who had invited me and that he had no say in the matter.

After quietly asking Boyfriend to calm down long enough for me to talk with Daughter, I asked her whether she was willing to work with Oscar, or did she want this stressful situation to continue? Did she wish to allow Boyfriend to go on screaming at and roughing up *her* dog, or would she rather defuse the charged atmosphere in the home that revolved around Oscar but probably had nothing to do with him. I suggested that it would be safer *not* to jerk him around the neck, wrestling him to the floor with blows and kicks, because one day he may decide that he's had enough and retaliate. Boyfriend started screaming again that if Oscar ever harmed him, he was a dead dog. Daughter started to cry, Mother was screaming at Boyfriend, and I was wondering what did I ever do to the wonderful veterinarian who referred them to me to deserve this? This had all the elements of a nightmare, and the only way Father kept his sanity was by tuning out his family.

From sheer exhaustion, Daughter and Boyfriend departed from the room. I was left with Mother, Father, and Oscar. We had a few quiet moments and I explained that unless they were willing to commit themselves to a little patient work and effort with Oscar, then the only responsible and ethical suggestion I could make was to find him a quiet home. He was a good dog, affectionate, intelligent, and willing to please, but he could not continue to go through such emotional battering coupled with physical abuse much longer. They agreed.

Then, Daughter finally got upset enough to inform Boyfriend that Oscar was *her* dog and she would be the one to decide his fate. Now I could proceed to demonstrate to Daughter how to work with Oscar, and to her amazement, the correct commands worked again! It did take a few seconds for Oscar to respond, but she accepted this. After all, Oscar was not a pro-grammed robot!

Mother made the only perceptive observation addressing Boyfriend: "Oscar behaves like you because you created the problem. He howls like you, he is stubborn like you, intractable like you, and has no self-control like you. The only difference is that Oscar is more intelligent and more sensitive than you because as Mrs. Yarden showed us all, he is willing and able to learn, and you are not!"

When I called back two months later to follow up on Oscar, I was informed that Boyfriend was gone, no longer a part of their life. Oscar became a sweet, calm, and responsive dog.

THE HOLIDAY VICTIMS

Many people look forward to the annual holidays, planning the decorations, gift giving, parties, and guests. There will be joyous noise and excitement in the house, and also stress of various kinds. In all the hubbub, don't forget your pet!

Do not leave a plugged in electrical wire around the Christmas tree when you leave your pet alone. Depending on the animal's age and curiosity, he may knock the tree over, but at least he will not electrocute himself, set the house on fire, or die from smoke inhalation. Hanukkah candles pose the same hazard, so constant vigilance is essential.

Parties are an integral part of the holidays and they are fun. It is, however, not absolutely essential to include your pet in the revelries. To many animals such noise and excitement are chaotic and very unsettling. This applies especially to those who are not used to large crowds, are easily excited, and those who are not expert in the art of getting out from under many feet, or who are barkers with a tendency to be on the hysterical side. At least cats can escape to high places when the going gets rough and stay out of the way—dogs rarely have that option.

Some people do not accept the fact that it is *not* funny or cute to feed good-ies to their pet (if the party is at your house, to *your* pet), including alcohol. There is nothing funny either about blowing smoke into an animal's face just to see him gag and choke! Place Chester in a quiet part of the house like the bedroom, with his bed, food, water, and toys. Leave on a light, soft classical music or television, and visit him from time to time to make sure that he is safe and does not feel excluded and rejected. Don't forget his toilet needs! If any of your *sensible* guests wish to see him, let them do so (one or two at a time) and spend a few quiet, affectionate minutes with him throughout the evening.

Giving dogs as Christmas gifts is *a bad idea* and is *dangerous to the dog*, in spite of the emotional appeal we are bombarded with by the media. This is **not** the time to bring home a confused, frightened, or very young dog. Instead, give a gift certificate or a promissory note to be honored *after* the holidays, and *allow the recipient to select the dog.* This method is far more responsible and successful. It may also insure that the dog will not be resented later.

The temptation to show off a puppy is almost irresistible, but what he *needs most* is quiet, rest, reassurance, and a chance to get to know his new family and environment. He is away from his mother and siblings for the first time in his life in a place he doesn't know with people he doesn't know. This can be scary and confusing.

Newly acquired adult animals also need quiet, affection, reassurance, and time to familiarize themselves with their new surroundings and new family. Excitement and noise, tension and lack of rest, being passed from person to person are all counterproductive to their adjustment to the new home. Animals easily react to such chaos with what *appears* to be antisocial and even hostile behavior—a prelude to disaster.

Have a wonderful time during the holiday season, but allow your dog to enjoy herself, too, calmly and safely. Include her in your family's activities and fun but keep her from the hubbub and chaos. Protect her from decorations, from doors left carelessly or accidentally open by guests, and from other disasters by vigilance and supervision.

BIRTH CONTROL AND BREEDING

Millions of dogs are deliberately killed in the United States every year because there are no homes for them. But these millions are all "mongrels" and mutts, people may say, as if that were an excuse. After all, no one would deliberately kill a purebred dog, right? Wrong! Go to any pound or animal shelter, either publicly or privately funded, and take a look at the purebred animals slated for and executed day after day, year after year. This obscene situation developed in part because of uncontrolled backyard breeding. There are almost as many reasons for allowing uncontrolled, back-yard breeding as there are dogs killed. Some of my favorites are:

1. *"It is against nature to spay and neuter dogs.* However, people "go against" nature to domesticate dogs and keep them as pets.

2. *"It is against God's law to interfere with any creature's body in this manner."* But it is not against God's law to allow mass slaughter of his creatures, through this kind of non-interference?

3. *"I give them away free to good homes."* It would be more kind and sensible to value them instead of passing them out like disposable items. Often such breeders don't follow up on the "good homes" they send them to.

4. *"I want my children to witness the miracle of birth."* But would you allow your children to witness the kind of miracle of birth they can really relate to—the birth of a human child?

5. *"If I leave them on the side of the road in the country, a good-hearted farmer will give them a home."* How many good-hearted farmers can there be?

6. *"Dogs always survive on the streets, so will these."* They do *not* survive on the streets. They die of hunger, thirst, disease, and car accidents.

7. *"The pounds always find homes for them."* Pounds are lucky if they find homes for two out of ten (according to animal control or the SPCA).

8. *"Private shelters never put them to sleep."* Yes, they do! They don't have unlimited space or resources to keep them all.

9. *"It wasn't my fault—a male dog jumped the fence when Sugar was in heat."* Actually, it *was* your fault! If Sugar had been spayed, the male dog probably would not have jumped the fence in the first place.

10. *"I enjoy sex and want my pets to have their fun, too."* The difference is that your sexual activity does not result in pregnancy every time you indulge. A dog or a cat does get pregnant every time. *Enjoyment in human terms does not apply to dogs.*

Birth control is easy, relatively inexpensive, and permanent. You don't have to worry about accidental or unwanted pregnancies. For those readers who resist sterilization of male pets, here is a letter written by Dr. Thomas E. Vice, DVM. When I spoke with him not too long ago, he stated that what he said in the letter is more important today than ever.

"It is my recommendation that male dogs be castrated. This suggestion almost always meets with client resistance, but castration of the male dog has definite beneficial effects, both biological and psychological. First, let us examine the psychological aspect, which has its origin in the basic, biological sex drive.

"The female dog while 'in heat' emits an odor (pheromones) that attracts male dogs from long distances. (*This is irresistible!*) It is a rare area in any city in which this sexual stimulus is not repeatedly present for the male dog, whether he is allowed to run loose or is confined to a house or yard.

"As a result, the male dog is constantly being stimulated with virtually no outlet for his very strong biological drive. It is not uncommon for these dogs to become irritable and develop undesirable habits such as breaking housetraining, mounting the children, guests, furniture, or anything within their reach at their repeated attempts at masturbation. The male dog is thus actually in a constant state of nervous agitation.

"This leads up to the biological aspect of the problem. As a result of this constant stimulation without natural and logical relief, male dogs very frequently develop infections of the prepuce, prostatic hypertrophy, or other lower genito-urinary problems. Many times these are low grade and are undetected by the owner. These problems, in turn, frequently lead to more serious kidney disease, which in male dogs five years of age or older is probably the most common disease seen in most small animal veterinary practices. Kidney disease is far more common in the male dog than the female. Consequently it is my contention that castration, early in the male dog's life (six to seven months) will prevent many, if not all of these problems."

At the risk of being accused of being sexist and calling only for the neutering of male dogs, let us look at the advantages of spaying females. In their case it is also not merely a question of birth control but a matter of their health, quality of life, and longevity.

Many people (including veterinarians, believe it or not!) are under the impression that allowing a female to have one oestrus cycle is good because it "calms her down." The fact is that a heat cycle does not calm her down, it makes her edgy, nervous, and stressed, and she will seek mates. Another commonly held idea is that by allowing her to have one litter, she will be more mature.

Both are myths! By allowing a female to have one heat cycle, you are increasing her chances of developing breast cancer in later life, usually around five to six years of age. As for maturity, I am always amused when I hear this from a couple who is childless. I look at them and ask the husband, "Is your wife immature and restless?" The answer is always no. Then I suggest that their female dog will also reach maturity and a calm state of being with proper education, a good quality of life, understanding, love, and affection. It is not medically indicated that a pregnancy will give her these—only time and her human partners can do it.

By not spaying a female, there are serious risks involved: uterine cancer, pyometra, cervical cancer, breast cancer, and repeated false pregnancies, to name a few. Spaying will protect her from these, keep her young and healthy, and it will lengthen her life.

DESIGNER DOGS

I find ear cropping, tail docking, and other dog "fashions" ugly and cruel. Fortunately, more and more owners refuse to put their pets through such painful misery.

There is *never* any health reason for cropping a dog's ears. This is being attested to by more and more veterinarians. In England the procedure is illegal. In Germany it has not been practiced for several decades. Such surgery does not improve the quality of life for the dog. Moreover, owners are relieved when they find that ear cropping and tail docking are *not required* except by the parent breed clubs (albeit with cooperation of the AKC).

Advocates of these barbaric practices will tell you that cropped ears and docked tails are essential so that the dogs do not tear or hurt them as they work. Yet how many of our pets work? "Cropped ears make a Doberman look *mean,*" an advocate might say. But a Doberman *is* a Doberman with untouched ears, and his protective nature does not disappear because no one tortured him. He will be a lot calmer and stress-free if his essential body parts are left alone.

The dog's ears and tail are essential tools of communication, vital parts necessary for body language. He can talk to you (and other dogs) with ears and tail eloquently and clearly. To see the stubs of these appendages trying to "talk" always saddens me.

On the other hand, dogs with hair over their eyes can use a trim in order to communicate better. This procedure won't hurt them but it *will* help them. I find nervous, easily startled Old English Sheepdogs, Shih Tzus, Lhasa Apsos, Yorkshire Terriers, and others whose problem is that hair obstructs their vision. The argument that the hair is necessary to protect their eyes from dust and foreign objects does not make sense for most of these dogs who live in condos, apartments, luxurious houses with yards, and homes where they don't herd sheep, they don't hunt, and they are never in the field. Instead, they can collect grasses, foxtails, and other harmful things in the hair, which can cause serious problems. Once the owner gets the hair around the eyes clipped, the dog looks around in wonder, and the owner is delighted to find a pair of beautiful, expressive eyes looking back at him.

Designer dogs, cropped and docked dogs are simply mutilated dogs. Hopefully, the practice will die out and our vanities will not have to be vicariously catered to by our pets' suffering.

CHAPTER

12

Old Age and Saying Good-bye

Wouldn't it be wonderful if we could have a dog who would have a life expectancy of 60 years? If it were possible we could put off the infirmities of old age in our pets and would not have to go through the sadness of watching them ail, weaken and die all too soon, not to mention the wretchedness of having to make the decision to ease them into death gently, painlessly, mercifully—and *never* alone.

However, dogs age as we do. The smaller the breed the longer the life span, and the larger the breed, the shorter they live. While small Poodles, Yorkies, Beagles, and Random breeds can live to the ripe age of 19 to 20 years, Great Danes, Irish Wolfhounds, Mastiffs, Newfoundlands, and the like are considered old at the age of seven to eight years with a life expectancy of, at most, ten to eleven years.

Old animals have certain physical needs that are quite different from when they were young and in their prime. Isn't it the same with us? Their nutritional requirements, exercise regime, protection against the elements, the need for more rest and quiet, diminishing vision and hearing, and even change in appetite must all be taken into consideration. Their emotional needs also change and they often cannot and will not be bothered with all the nonsense they accepted from us with humor and tolerance when they were young. This is payback time! We pay back with compassion and patience for the pleasure and love they gave us all their lives.

This may not be the time to stress a canine senior citizen with a highly active, bouncy puppy. Some will accept such aggravation, but many will not or would rather not. My Golden Retriever/Puli was the best natured dog I have ever met. At the age of seven she was presented with a tiny, eight-week-old Smooth English Fox Terrier, Aurora. Taffy not only accepted the little handful, she mothered her devotedly, tolerated the ear-chewing, leg-nipping, tail-chasing, hanging on, and the general mayhem a vigorous puppy is capable of dishing out. She educated Aurora in courtesy, good manners and housetraining and provided her with a soft, warm and secure lap whenever the baby needed reassurance and rest.

Six years later, when a third puppy desperately needed a home and I took her in, Taffy had little patience, little tolerance, and almost no interest in the new baby. She refused to play, and if Pip approached her bouncing and inviting play, she would retreat. If retreat was not possible, she would emit a quiet but ominous growl to inform the little one that she was to be left in peace. In fairness to the aging Taffy, I came to the rescue by vigilance and care so that her well-earned and well-deserved rest was not disturbed. Instead I encouraged the friendship between Circe (Aurora's successor) and the new pup, which worked out extremely well.

When we bring a new puppy home, it is very difficult to imagine that he or she will die before we do and the time to part will be upon us. Much as we thrust the thought away, it will have to be faced and dealt with. Accidental death of a pet is a shock and the death of a young pet or of one in the prime of life is very difficult to deal with. Death due to old age is perhaps a little easier on the one hand, only because it is natural and inevitable. On the other hand, having been together for many years the old dog's death leaves a raw, gaping hole in our lives.

There was a time when grieving over the death of a pet was viewed by most people as an exaggerated emotion not worthy of human expression. Today, the loss of a companion animal and the ensuing grief and desire to mourn are better understood.

However, we not only recognize and approve of grieving for a pet (which is as it should be), but we tend to go too far. In a recent rash of books and articles, we are even *taught how* to grieve and mourn for a lost companion. I am *not* minimizing the emotional battering we take when we lose a beloved pet. How can I when in my work with clients I do bereavement counseling (read "consoling") and see the pain and the heartache owners experience at such a time? I practically "sit shivah" in mourning for each and every companion animal I lose. What I *am* saying is that grief counseling for pet owners is not always necessary as lots of books would have you believe. I find that most people want to be left alone to grieve in private. Time, understanding, and compassion from family and friends is usually all the help grieving pet owners need. For those who desire help, it is available, but don't accept that you must have it, otherwise you are not grieving appropriately.

When an owner makes the necessary decision to euthanize a pet because it is the only kind thing left to do, too often there is a delayed reaction of denial, guilt, anger, and deep sorrow, which is seen by some as exaggerated or misplaced. Well-meaning friends or relatives may even tell the owner that he shouldn't feel such feelings. Too often, the grieving person is presented with a new pet "to replace the other" when he is not ready. However, a beloved companion animal can *never* be replaced. So, with the introduction of a new pet too soon, the grieving of the old pet is not completed, and both human and animal have difficulty developing a rapport. The following case had all these elements. The client had a very difficult time dealing with her feelings of grief and saying good-bye. The resulting stress was affecting her remaining pet, and in the erroneous belief that *only her dog was mourning,* she called for help.

CASE OF THE GRIEVING SAMOYED

Scarlett was a five-year-old intact female Samoyed whose mate Rhett died at the age of 11 after a losing battle with cancer. She became listless, withdrawn, disinterested, lost her appetite, and refused to play. Her walks, which she used to enjoy, now consisted of going out to eliminate and then turning homeward again where she could retreat to a corner of the bedroom and stay there. After a thorough medical examination that revealed no physical problems (except a slight weight loss), her owner called me to consult about Scarlett.

When I arrived, Scarlett was nowhere to be seen. I was greeted in a very friendly manner by Jake, a three-year-old intact male Samoyed who, as it turned out, was Scarlett's and Rhett's son. He was adopted by friends, but when Rhett died they returned him to make the loss easier to bear. Scarlett was in the bedroom in her corner and when I entered, she lifted her head, let me stroke her but remained where she was. We stayed in the bedroom with her and when we finally coaxed her onto the bed, she lay there with her head on her owner's lap.

I got the background on both animals. Rhett was acquired at the age of eight weeks and he was six when he took the six-month-old Scarlett to his heart. When she was three, they became the proud parents of four beautiful, healthy pups. Rhett and Scarlett were very close and affectionate with each other, both gentle and dedicated parents and enjoyed a close bond and rapport with their owner.

Recent events were recounted. In the beginning of September, cancer was diagnosed in Rhett, and although not much hope was offered, surgery was

requested and performed. Rhett gained a little time, but soon after Thanksgiving it became obvious that the disease had the upper hand. Just before Christmas Rhett was admitted to the hospital again where no further help was possible. He became very weak and began to experience pain.

Because of the large number of guests in her home, the *owner was not present* when Rhett was euthanized at her request to spare him more pain.

Because of the holidays she did not have the time—or unconsciously did not make the time—to deal with Rhett's death. When I visited her in February, she was still talking about it in short, clipped sentences, tensely chain smoking. Whenever her eyes would fill with tears, she would immediately choke them back. It was about that time that she noticed the change in Scarlett.

Rather than talk about Scarlett, I guided the conversation to the owner's feelings and thoughts about Rhett.

"Tell me, what did Rhett mean to you? Who was he in your life?"

"He was my best friend, my child, my loyal partner, and my most uncritical and loving companion."

"How did you feel when he died?"

"I felt more devastated than when I lost a human family member. I guess that's a bit sick..."

"Well, if you consider that Rhett *was* all the things to you that you described, and he *was* all those things to you for *11 years*, tell me why you think it is sick?"

"But that's what my friends have been saying—that it was a bit sick to feel this way about an animal..."

"Tell me something. How many relationships in your life can you compare to the special one you had with Rhett? How many were as loving, loyal, uncritical, devoted, and above all, as unchanging and durable?"

"Actually none. Very few human relationships in my life can compare to the special bond we had—not forgetting Scarlett, of course."

"If all that is true, then how do you really feel about his death?"

"I feel empty, miserable, and lost. I feel angry at myself, angry at Rhett, and guilty. The void he left can't be filled by his son."

"Let's talk about your guilt and anger at yourself. Why do you feel those?"

"Because if I had been more careful, more aware, more alert, I could have helped him. I could have taken him to the doctor sooner and he might still be alive. It is probably my fault..."

"But hasn't your veterinarian explained to you that the kind of cancer Rhett had develops and spreads extremely fast? That there was nothing you could have noticed or seen or done about it?"

"Yes, he did."

"Then let's look at your anger at Rhett."

"I know it's stupid, but I am angry that he died and left me; that I can't get over it and that the hurt won't ease at all."

"Look, the fact is that Rhett did not die for the purpose of deserting or abandoning you and causing you pain. You know that!"

"I know."

"Tell me something. Have you cried for him?"

"I'm trying not to because I've been told over and over that you don't mourn a dog as much as a human and that another dog will help. That's why I accepted Jake back. But he is not Rhett and even Scarlett knows it."

"Just because you were told that you shouldn't mourn a dog as much as a human, does that make the statement true? Are you able to stop feeling the pain and the deep loss? Can you stop the sorrow and the tears?"

"I'm trying."

"Why? You have been talking with me for an hour and during that time your eyes filled up at least six times. Rather than let the tears come, you choked them back. You also choked back your feelings because you were told by people who cannot fathom and understand the very feelings you cannot ignore. Does that make sense to you?"

"Not really."

"Then are you wondering why Scarlett is unhappy? The bond and the love between you and her is intact. Rhett's death did not change that, but as long as you refuse to relive your feelings and insist on maintaining this tension in yourself, you can't help but transmit them to her. That's what she is really suffering from—not that she does not feel Rhett's absence, but the unreconciled stress you are experiencing is felt by her too, very deeply."

"You mean that I am doing it to her?"

"No, of course you are not 'doing it to her.' There is no place here for more guilt and blame. What I *am* saying is that she feels not only the loss of Rhett but also *the loss of you*. Until you deal with your own grief, you are holding yourself remote from her. That's what troubles her more than anything else."

"What I really want to do is cry my heart out!"

"Then ask yourself this: After all you told me about Rhett, your best friend, companion, child, loving partner, is he worth crying for?"

"Yes, he is!"

"In that case, why not use my shoulder and let the tears come? Feel again all that happened, the worry and the fear and the sorrow and the loss. I think you could use a hug just about now anyway."

She did use my shoulder and was finally able to cry. She relived all that happened, all the feelings she tried to deny at the urging of well-meaning but mistaken friends. She realized that her guilt feelings were compounded by her absence when euthanasia was performed. She thought of all the places Rhett liked and how empty they were without him, of coming home and not seeing his happy face. After a while, Scarlett raised her head, got closer, and licking her face, began to console her. In a little while my shoulder was no longer needed and she was weeping with Scarlett in her arms. They were mourning Rhett's death, for the first time, together.

In about an hour the crying subsided and we left the bedroom. Over a welcome cup of coffee we discussed the relief she felt for the first time since Rhett's illness and death. During the conversation, so quietly that the owner did not notice, Scarlett appeared in the living room and was now sitting at the sliding door where Rhett used to sit, watching the birds outside. Although I saw her coming I said nothing because I wanted the owner to discover Scarlett herself. Jake greeted his mother effusively and for the first time since his arrival, she actually took notice of him.

When I left, Scarlett accompanied me to the door like a gracious hostess. The owner called me several more times and we talked about her feelings and about Rhett. By the middle of March, Scarlett's behavior was back to normal, her appetite improved, she gained back the weight she had lost and was busy teaching her son good manners and social graces.

The owner also felt better. She was now able to talk about Rhett with loving reminiscence, mention his name without choking on it, and even recount his silly antics with a chuckle. She still cried occasionally but the sharp pain turned into a dull ache. Her anger was gone and her guilt was eased considerably. She was content to let Rhett rest in peace, and Jake's close resemblance to his late father was a source of gladness instead of a bitter reminder.

Since the sense of loss is a highly complex emotion—be it family member or a companion animal—the first thing to concede is that a loss is a loss regardless of the number of legs or the length of the ears. It is an acute pain and many owners mourn the loss of their companion animals more deeply and longer that that of a human relative—not because they are "anti-human," unfeeling or callous, but because they received more unconditional acceptance, loyalty, devotion, and emotional support from their pet.

It is hard to adjust to the death of a friend one has cared for, lived with and loved for more than a dozen years. Yet adjustment is essential because the only alternative is to crawl into a hole and stay there. Even the deceased animal would object to such denial of his life and the enjoyment he gave while living. At this stage, one must believe that the pain will lessen and although it may never leave, one can come out of the grieving process whole, and able to go on.

Often, people who lose a beloved pet never get another because "I can't go through this again." Of course they can't go through "this" again—considering that they haven't gone through "this" in the first place. It is also they who suffer the most. As for being able to stand the pain—there is no free lunch! If Chester was worth having and loving, then he is worth hurting for.

For some owners the grieving process takes longer than for others. There are those whose aching hearts and empty arms are ready almost immediately for a warm and wriggly little body with an appealing face. Others need time to part from the old companion before they are ready to give their hearts and commit themselves to a new relationship. Each individual must follow his or her instincts and not be either slowed or rushed in any way.

Unfortunately, this is the point in the grieving process that is often made counterproductive by friends with the best of intentions who are apt to say something as deeply hurtful as "it was just a dog" or "you can always get another." Some get bored and tired of hearing about the deceased pet and wonder why the owner "carries on so."

On the other side of the coin, friends who have been through such loss will know exactly what you are feeling, will encourage you to talk and remember the lost pet, will smile with you, shed a tear with you, or just simply hold you while you are weeping. When you can't talk to a friend, you might try writing about your feelings. This helped me as I mourned the loss of my dog Nefer. Here's what I wrote:

Nefer died last Friday. She left an emptiness that can never be filled. She had her own place in my life and I walk with the sharp pain of her death and my heart will always house an ache for her. Yet the sorrow of her loss is eased by the precious gift of the eight years she gave me.

I found Nefer abandoned in a hellhole, a boarding kennel where she spent the first year of her life in a small, cramped cage. A broken leg was left untreated, forced to lie in her own waste, emaciated from lack of food and terrified of the world. Her terror eased after some time with me but it never quite disappeared. She never had a puppyhood. She never learned to play. She never did any of the delightful, aggravating, charming, and annoying things growing puppies do. She was a year old when I managed to release her from her solitary confinement but that one year aged her far beyond what she should have been.

When I brought her home she was full of fears—of humans, animals, noises, open spaces, swooping birds and falling leaves . . . if any of my other dogs as much as looked at her food at meal times, she backed away, too fearful to eat. So Nefer had her special place where she ate, with me sitting near her and she looking up to make sure I was there. She was ill with chronic colitis and on medication and special diets all her life. It was no hardship for me to adjust to her needs and when she taught herself to ask for my attention by tapping me gently with her paw—it was a happy achievement for both of us.

She had courage, valor, patience, and endurance. Although lame, she was never lazy or indolent. She was as protective as a lioness—all forty golden pounds of her—a formidable alarm-giver, she threatened anyone she perceived dangerous to me. Yet she never harmed a soul! She accepted me immediately and eventually all the other animals of my home and heart. She accepted five kittens patiently, agreeably, and with courtesy and grace.

She had cancer and was in pain. I had to make the decision to give her the last gift of love, the gift of a gentle death. And while the decision to stop her pain was easy, the deed was the hardest. It always is. The last words I whispered in her ear as she lay in my arms were "I'm glad I got you" because I whispered those same words into her ear every night of her life before she fell asleep on the love seat next to my bed.

She left me her love and her trust, her infinite gentleness and patience, her velvet-soft eyes, the sunshine of her coat and the pride of her elegant, slender head. She left me the memory of her attempts to play without really knowing how, the touch of her paw on my arm and the feel of her body curled up next to me.

Nefer died last Friday. And I'm glad I got her . . .

Children are a little different. Very young children deal with the death of a pet with greater ease and acceptance. They do miss the dog and have a hard time understanding death, but that's what makes it easier for them. They tend to be able to accept a new pet more quickly than adults are. They do not betray the old pet when they transfer their affection to the new pet, they just deal with their loss in a simpler way.

Children of preteen years face a different problem again. Some develop very close ties with their pets and depend on them for love and acceptance. The pets are confidants, sleeping partners, and at time, siblings. This may be the first time that a child of this age is confronted not only with her pet's death but with her own mortality—"If Sunshine can die, so can I." She may be reluctant to enter into a new friendship in order to protect herself.

Many bereaved owners find it healing to get involved in volunteer work in shelters, rescue, grooming, or helping with adoptions. Such work can be a wonderfully fulfilling bridge to the time when you are ready to accept and care for another pet. Until we accept that the pleasure we got from our deceased pet was so fulfilling that we can not live without it—we are not ready, and accepting a new pet is not fair to the pet nor to you. When the time is right, give your heart again and accept the joy another pet can give you.

Above all, when the new puppy or dog comes along, give him every chance to be all he can be. Don't compare him to the one you lost and don't look for the old in the new. Such feelings influence one's attitude and the pup will sense it. Let the departed friend rest in peace and go on with life and the most enjoyable business of building a brand new, wonderful partnership with your new friend and companion.

Conclusion

One of the most prevalent attitudes of trainers, behaviorists, and owners toward companion animals—even today—is punishment instead of management. The owner is still not likely to ask himself, "Why is my dog doing what he is doing?" Such a question is the basis of a philosophy or mind-set that can be summed us as, "Let's talk, let's use a language we can both comprehend, let's communicate and understand each other."

Instead, the tendency is for dog owners to threaten and to punish. Many trainers call this, euphemistically, "correction," and an incredible amount of vivid imagination has gone into inventing exotic means of such corrections. The best known, of course, are a large variety of leashes, chokers, pronged collars, sticks, rubber hoses, isolation, incarceration, electric shock, rolled up paper, hitting with hands, kicking, withdrawing privileges... The list is endless. This owner mind-set can be summed up as, "Pup, I demand that you do as I say or else I will hurt you!"

The idea of punishment seems to stem from child-rearing, in which bad deeds must be punished. This transference to animals has been enthusiastically endorsed by "experts" who maintain that "dogs do not understand." It has not been explained satisfactorily, however, that if they do *not* understand, then how is the correction effective?

This kind of attitude and conduct on the part of the owner is a sad mistake because the key to effective control and discipline of a companion animal is not punishment but education and management. Discipline means establishing limits and parameters and enforcing them consistently and clearly, without brutality or physical force (punishment).

With such management, the advantages are legion. The education and management method is more flexible, offers more options than a punitive approach, allows the owner to retain leadership, does not harm or destroy the relationship, does not create fear in the animal, which could culminate in retaliation, and most importantly, management is long-lasting and makes a permanent impression on the dog.

For the owner, the management approach eliminates frustration, tension, brutality, feelings of guilt, and inconsistency. Management is proactive and depends on foresight, understanding, internalizing, and planning. *It is a very good way to keep anger and impatience at bay and eventually eliminate them altogether*. **It is also a lot safer!**

Punishment, on the other hand, is confrontational, and the outcome is inevitably a win-lose or a lose-lose situation. Neither result is desirable because in either case, while the punishment may handle the immediate situation, it will either be ineffective next time, or a power struggle may evolve that will prepare the partners for the next incident. This will then create a cycle that is very difficult to break. Simply stated: Punishment will *stop* an unwanted behavior, but communication and education of the dog will *change* it.

I have met very few owners who did not feel a degree of guilt after they physically punished their dogs, or owners who allowed their pets exercise and play only as a privilege to be earned by good behavior. The confusion such methods create in the minds of dogs is no mystery. Without *teaching* the dog, without talking to the dog, such concepts will not make much sense. Even drug-sniffing dogs and search and rescue dogs who receive *play as a reward* for finding the target have been taught *why* they are rewarded!

Punitive methods of approach to a behavior problem prolong and promote testing on the part of the pup. More importantly, they prevent her from learning self-control. We *know* that a dog can be perfectly controlled on a choker at the end of a leash. But take the choker and leash off and *unless the pup was educated without it, she will not be able to control herself.* She doesn't have to! When it is required, the owner will again tether her to the leash and control will be taken from her.

Because of the negativity of punishment, it can easily damage the animal's self-respect and dignity, and prevent the development of her mental and emotional capabilities to their fullest. In too many cases the animal will retaliate—as any living being would when attacked or hurt—which may result in even more brutal handling, and unfortunately, even the death of the dog.

So talk to your pup and listen to him with your ears and with your eyes. Read his body language. If you give both of you a chance, you can learn how. *And let no one berate you for attributing human characteristics to your dog!* We all do it! I'll never forget the wonderful, caring, and emphatic veterinarian who told me that one of his dogs was a problem *child.* The other was a good *child.* He did have children of his own, but he understood and loved the human characteristics his companion animals had developed through close and loving association with him and his family.

Nevertheless, remember your dog is a dog, and that is as it should be. He enjoys being a dog, and has his own dignity and self-respect as a dog. Don't lose sight of the fact that although he has learned human characteristics, his *dog-hood* is important to him.

So love him, care for him, teach and educate him, enjoy him, but don't threaten, frighten, or hurt him, for any reason. Instead, communicate, observe, and determine why a problem is happening, and say, "Hey, Pup! Let's talk!"

Recommended Reading

Anderson, Moira K., *Coping with Sorrow,* Peregrine Press, 1987.

Bossard, J., "The Mental Hygiene of Owning a Dog," *Mental Hygiene,* v:28:408–413, 1944.

Burke, W. P., "Children's Thoughts, Reactions and Feelings Toward Dogs," *Journal of Psychology,* v.10:489, 1903.

Burnham, Patricia Gail, *Play Training Your Dog,* St. Martin's Press, 1980.

Campbell, William E., *Behavior Problem in Dogs,* Second Edition, AVP, 1991.

———, *Owners' Guide to Better Behavior in Dogs and Cats,* Alpine Press, 1986.

Fisher, John, *Think Dog,* Trafalgar Square Publishing, 1990.

———, *Why Does My Dog...?,* Howell Book House, 1991.

———, *Dogwise,* Souvenir Press, 1992.

Fox, Michael W., *Understanding Your Dog,* Bantam Books, 1974.

Griffin, Donald R., *The Question of Animal Awareness,* William Kaufmann, Inc., 1981 (revised and expanded edition).

———, *Animal Minds,* University of Chicago Press, 1992.

Herriott, James, *James Herriott's Dog Stories,* St. Martin's Press, 1986.

Hershhorn, Bernard S., *Active Years for Your Aging Dog,* Hawthorne Books, 1978.

Kirk, Douglas, *Canine Wickedness,* Morton Publishing Co., 1982.

Kowalski, Gary, *The Souls of Animals,* Stillpoint Publishing, 1991.

Lopez, Holstun, *Of Wolves and Men,* Charles Scribner & Sons, 1978.

McCaig, Donald, *Nop's Trials,* Warner Books, 1984.

Milani, Myrna, *The Invisible Leash,* New American Library, 1985.

———, *Body Language and Emotion of Dogs,* William Morrow & Co., 1986.

Moussaieff Masson, Jeffrey, *Dogs Never Lie About Love,* Crown Publishers, Inc., 1997.

Moussaieff Masson, Jeffrey, and Susan McCarthy, *When Elephants Weep,* Delacorte Press, 1995.

Mowat, Farley, *Never Cry Wolf,* Dell Publishing Co., 1963.

Moyer, K. E., *Physiology of Hostility,* Markham Publishing Co., 1971.

Pryor, Karen, *Don't Shoot the Dog: The Art of Teaching and Training,* Bantam Books, 1985.

Rollin, Prof. Bernard E., *Animal Rights and Human Morality,* Prometheus Books, 1981.

———, *The Unheeded Cry,* Oxford University Press, 1989.

Ryden, Hope, *God's Dog,* Viking Press, 1975.

Scott, J. P., *Animal Behavior,* University of Chicago Press, 1972.

Tanzer, H., *Your Dog Isn't Sick,* E.P. Dutton, 1977.

Index